The Toulouse-Lautrec Coloring Book

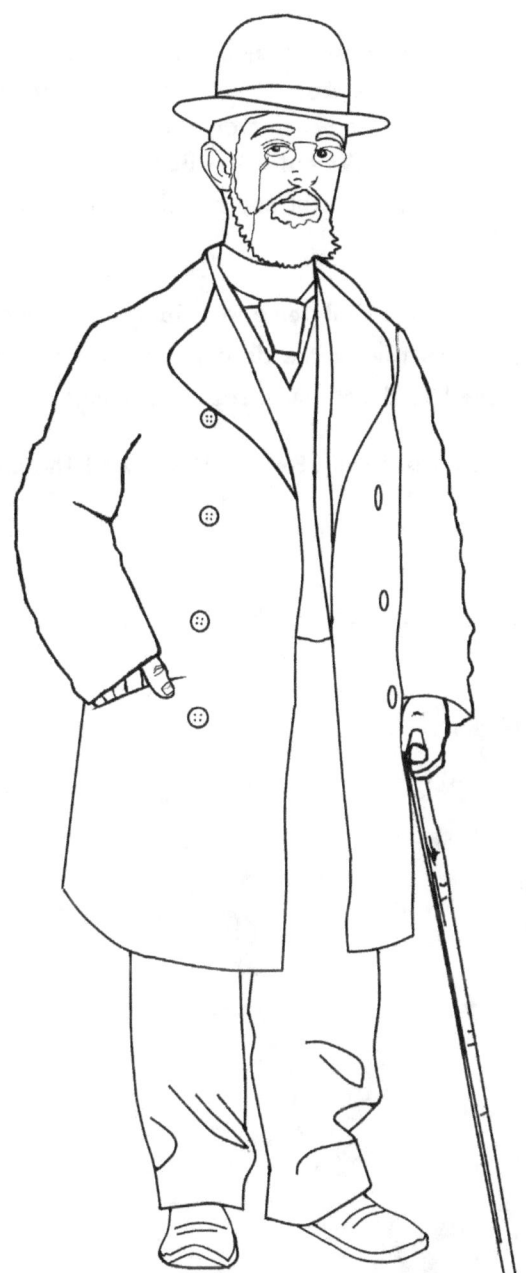

Henri de Toulouse-Lautrec
24 November 1864 – 9 September 1901

By A.T.LeMay

"Moulin Rouge" {Trans; Red Mill (windmill)}
"Concert bal tous les soirs" {Trans: Concert dance every night}

Lautrec created many posters advertising the Moulin Rouge. This poster was created in 1891. The woman in the painting is dancer Louise Weber (1866, - 1929). She nicknamed "La Goulue" {The Glutton} because she was known for quickly downing other peoples drinks.
The man in the painting is Valentin le désossé {Valentin the Boneless} (1843 - 1907). Valentin was given the nickname 'boneless' because of his graceful and complex contortions that he made with his hands and legs while dancing.

Valentin was the son of a wine merchant, his real name was Jacques Renaudin. He was a successful dance choreographer in Paris. Valentin was the maître de ballet (dance master) at the more upper class Bal Valentino and Bal Mabille. He loved to dance and refused payment at the Moulin Rouge.

Valentin was the dance partner of La Goulue from 1890 to 1895. And the couple are featured together in many of Lautrec's paintings and sketchs.

Original sketch

la Goulue et Valentin le désossé
{The Glutton and Valentin, the 'Boneless One'}

The Round shapes appear to be yellow gas lamps. In the days before electricity, Paris was one of the first cities to be lit by natural gas, an innovation that soon spread around the world. This is why Paris is still known as the city of light.

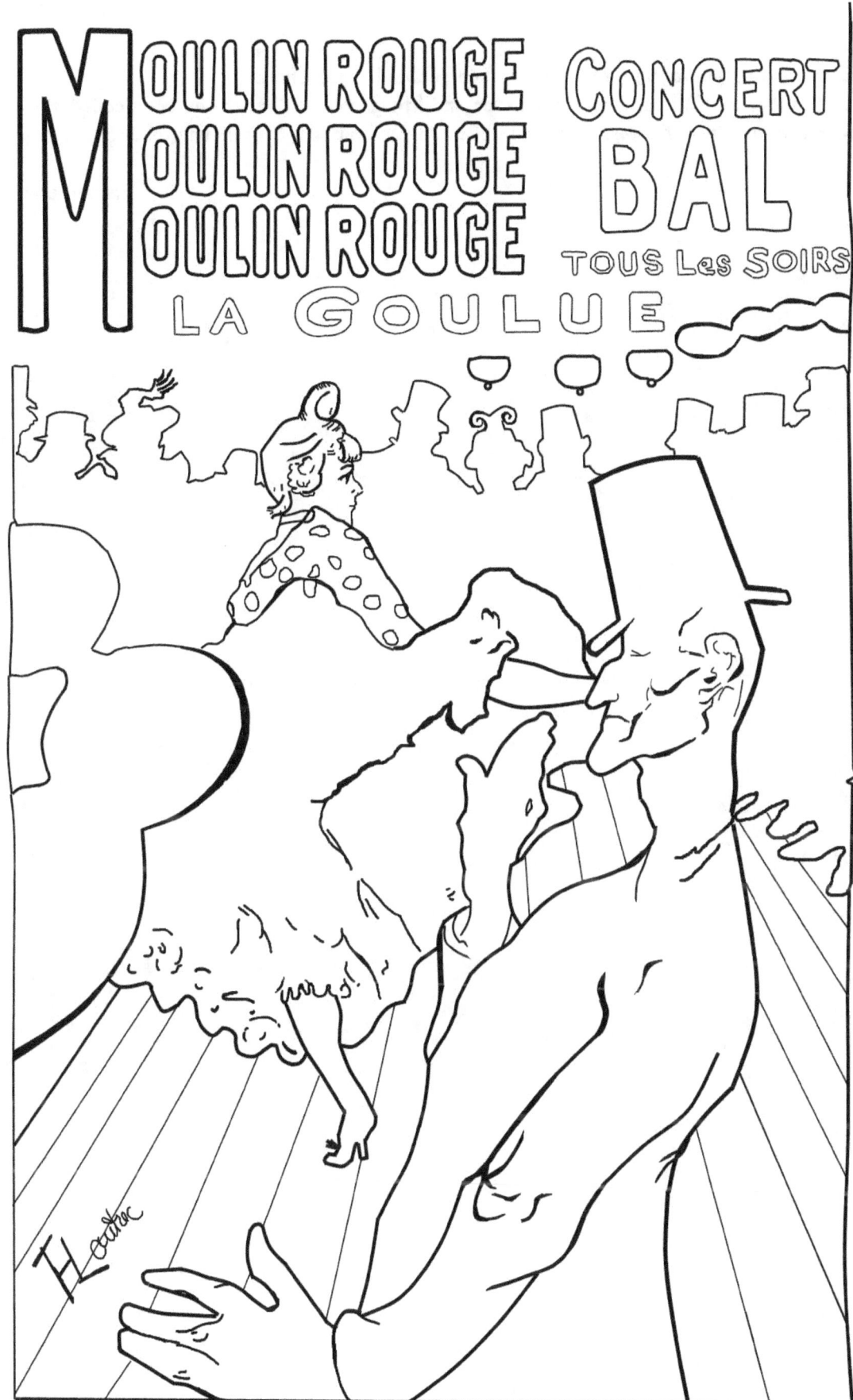

This picture is from of photograph of Toulouse Lautrec and Jules Chéret.
Jules Chéret (1836 – 1932) was a French painter and lithographer. Chéret has been called the father of the modern poster. Chéret's work was an inspiration for Lautrec. This is one of Chéret's posters for the Moulin Rouge .

From a photo 1892.

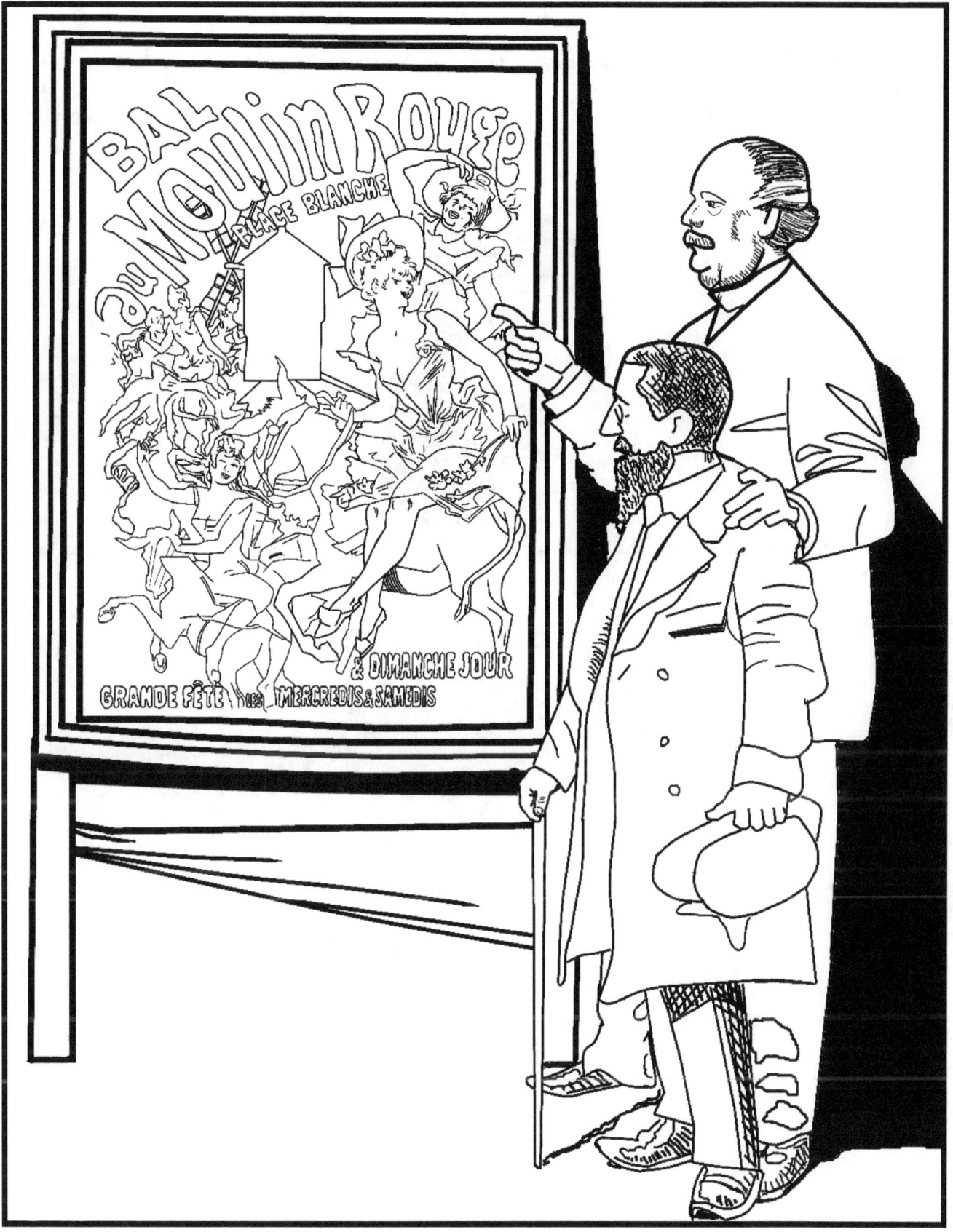

Jane Avril (1868-1943) was a singer and cancan dancer at the Moulin Rouge. She was a favorite subject of Lautrec's.

From an 1899 poster.

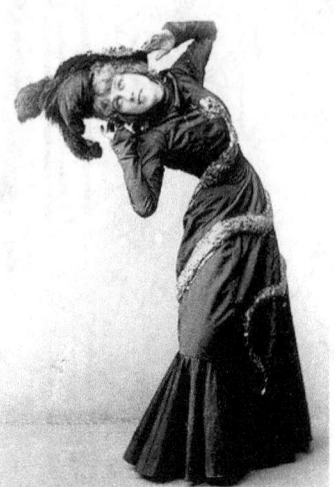

Lautrec sometimes made photographs of his subjects to capture their posture and gestures so that he could more easily draw and paint them.

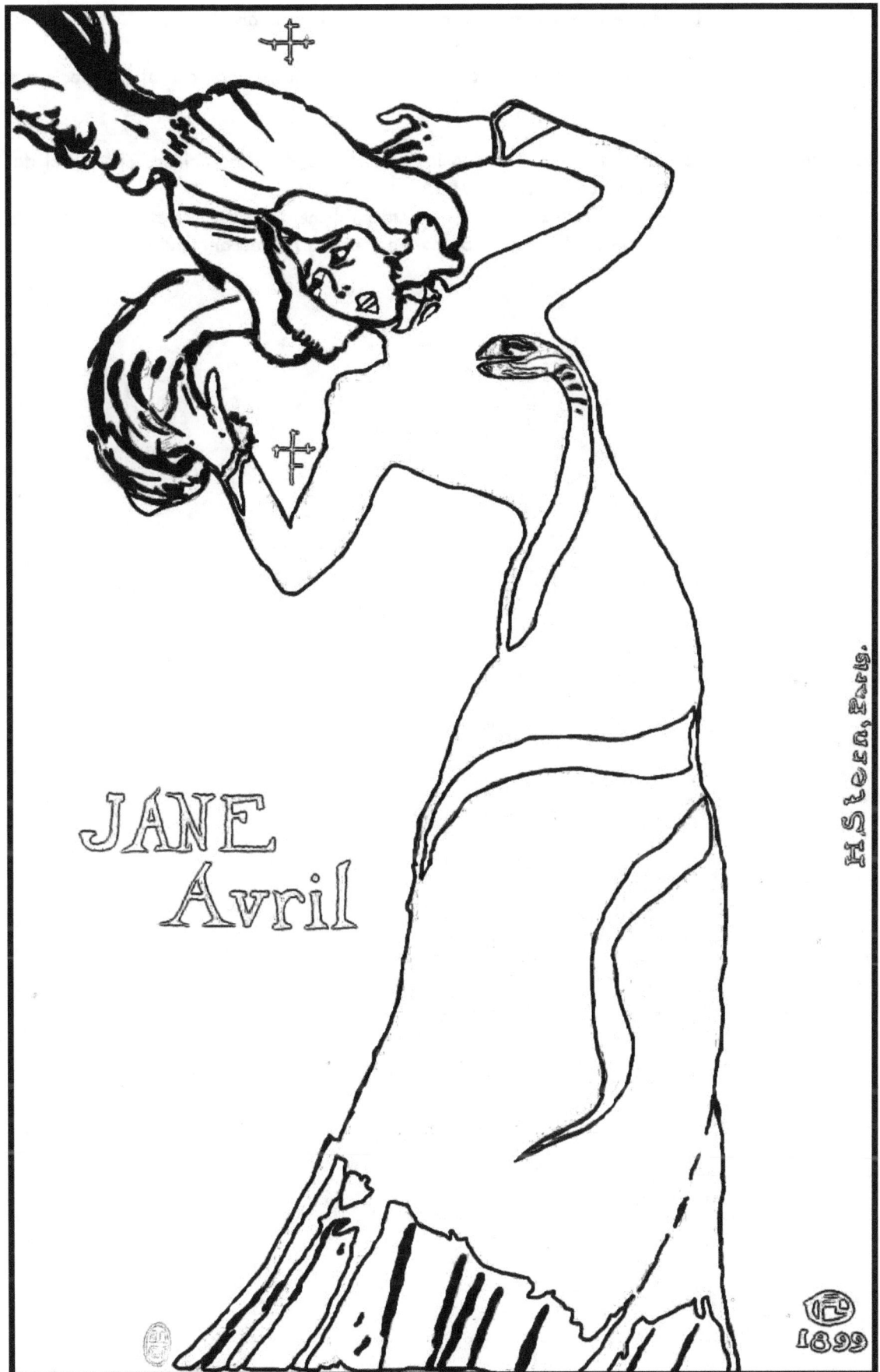

{Trans; Ambassador Aristide Bruant in his cabaret}

Aristide Bruant (1851 – 1925) was a cabaret singer and comedian. He became one of Lautrec's best friends in Paris.

Les Ambassadeurs was a restaurant in Paris, located in the luxurius Hôtel de Crillon. The Hôtel de Crillon was originally created by King Louis XV in 1758.
Les Ambassadeurs was well known in Lautrec's day as an entertainment center for the aristocracy. It was known then as a café-concert, or what would be called today a restaurant and nightclub.

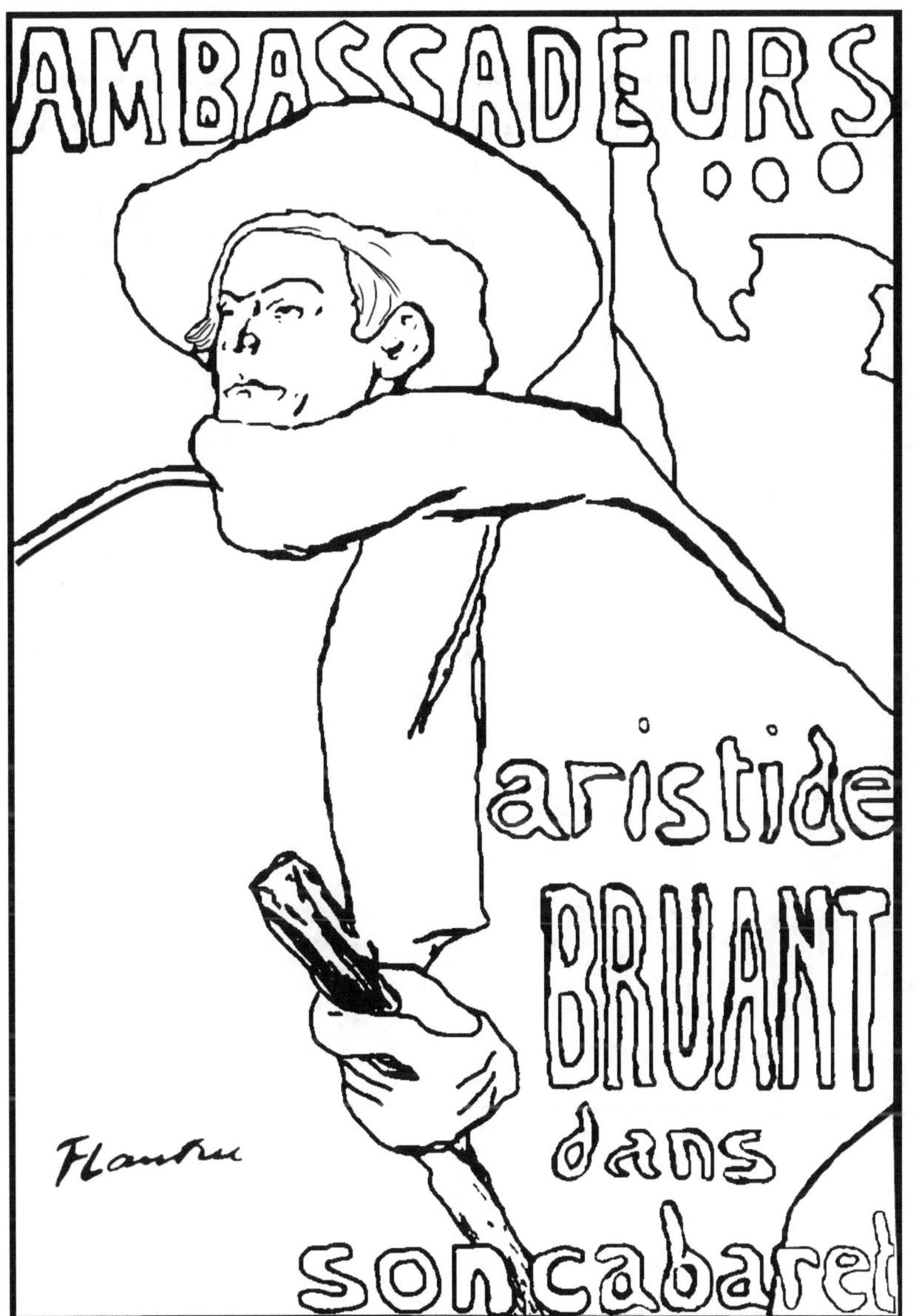

Lautrec created new printing processes for his posters advertising the Moulin Rouge. He also worked closely with the publication of several books and journals.
The lady in the print shop appears to be Jane Avril.

L'estampe originale publiée par le Journal des Artistes
{ The print original published by the journal of artists}

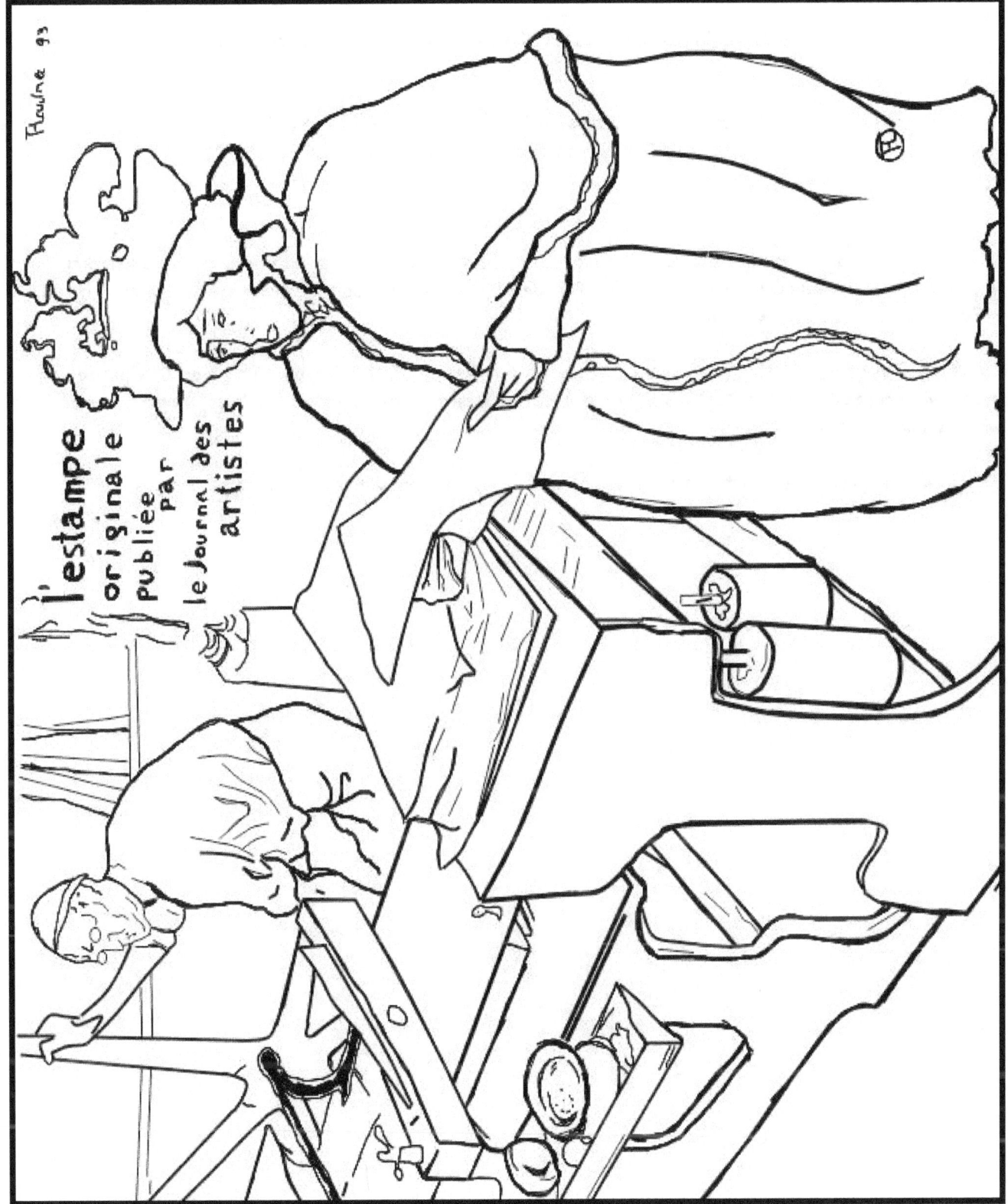

l'estampe
originale
publiée par
le Journal des
artistes

La Vache Enragée {The Mad Cow} a monthly Arts journal 1896

Journal mensuel illustre { Monthly illustrated journal}
Paris: 12f par an {Paris 12 francs per year}

In Paris there was in Lautrec's time there was an ancient celebration for butchers and meat workers known as La Promenade du Boeuf Gras {The Parade of the Fat Ox} During this festival butchers would parade through the city with live cattle.

La Vache Enragée {The Mad Cow} was a parody of the Parade of the Fat Ox. The Mad Cow parade was a carnival procession in the Paris bohemian district of Montmartre by artists, mimes, singers, dancer, writers and poets in 1896 and 1897.

The Mad Cow parade led to the publication of a monthly Arts magazine by the same name.

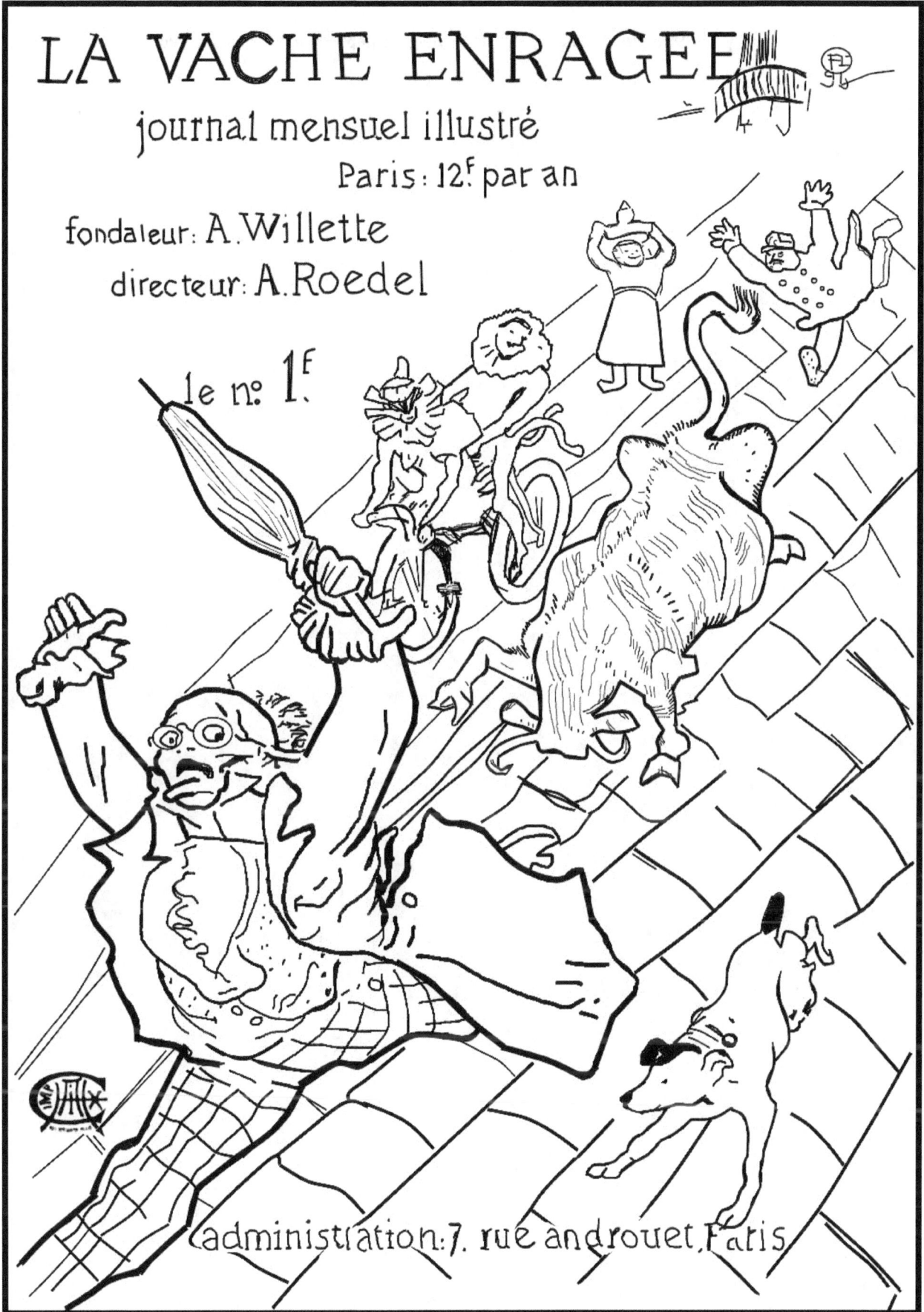

LA VACHE ENRAGEE

journal mensuel illustré

Paris : 12.ᶠ par an

fondateur : A. Willette

directeur : A. Roedel

le nᵒ 1ᶠ

administration : 7. rue androuet, Paris

"The Jockey" 1899. Horse racing has long been a popular past time in France.

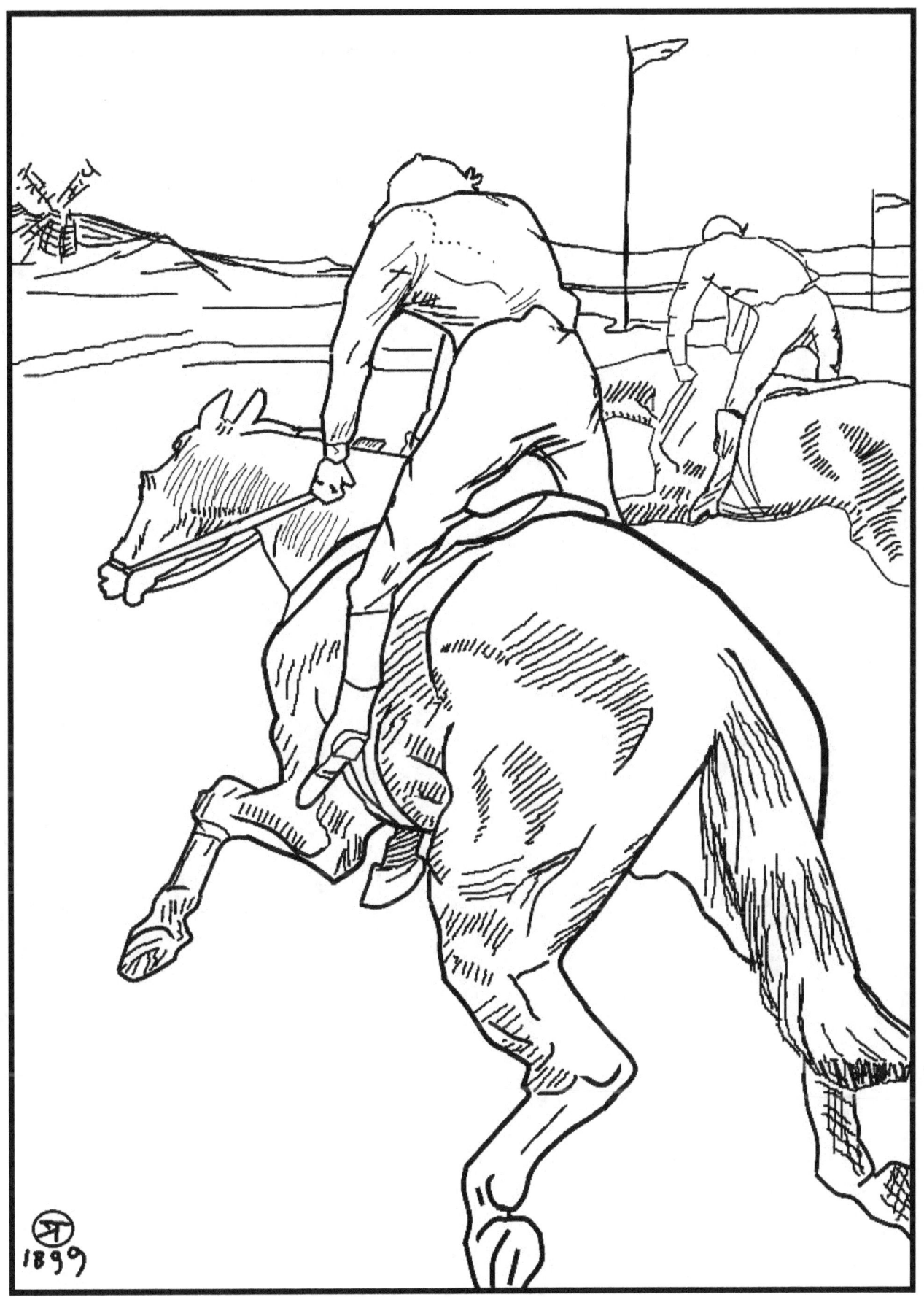

Rafael Padilla (1868-1917), known as Chocolat was a Cuban born dancer, singer and comedian who lived in Paris.

Chocolat Dancing in the Bar Darchille

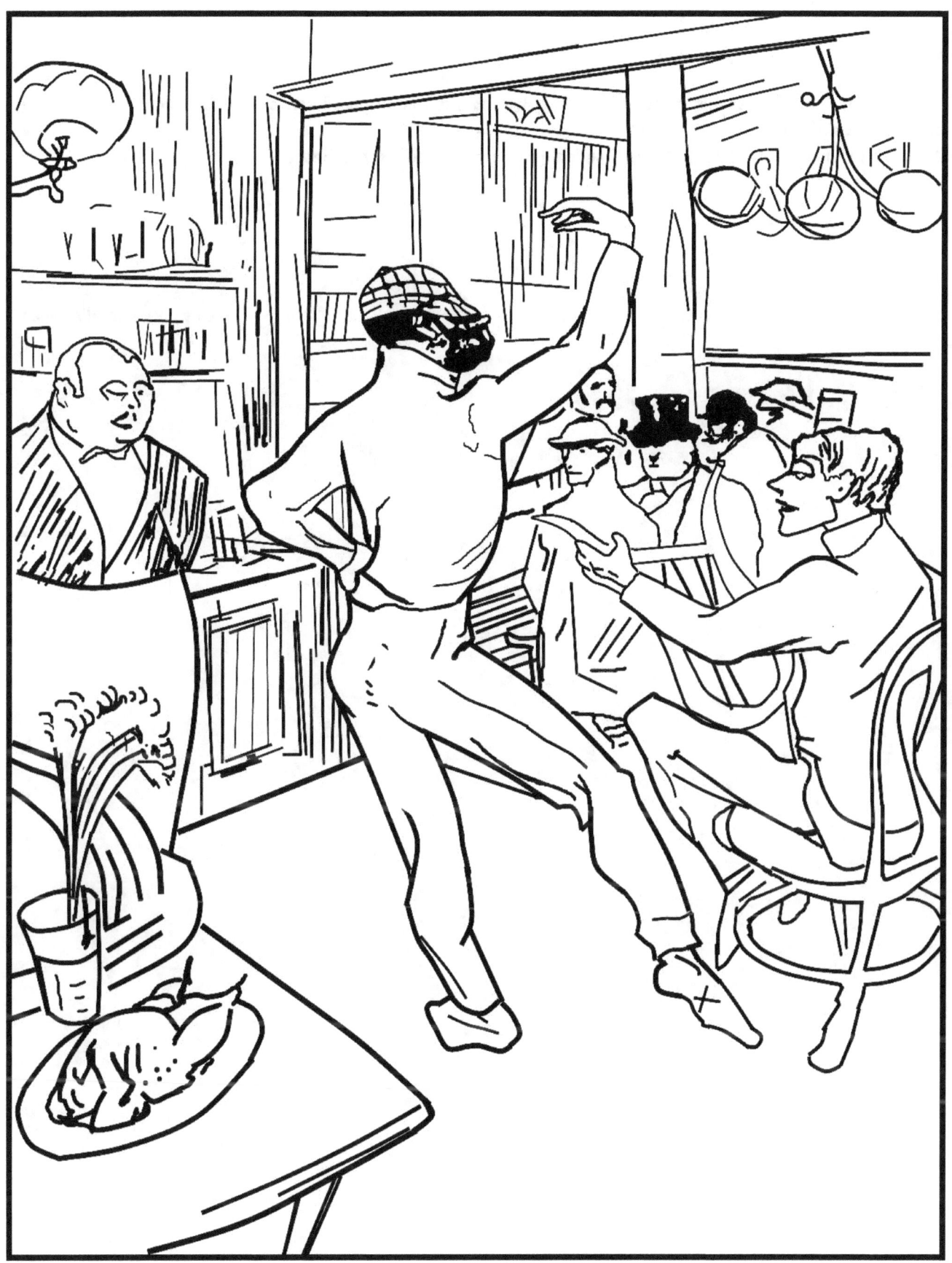

The cover of "Les Vielles Histoires" { The Old Stories } a collection of songs by poet Jean Goudezki and composer Désiré Dihau.
 Dihau is the man in the top hat and Goudezki is represented as the bear.

Les Vielles Histoires

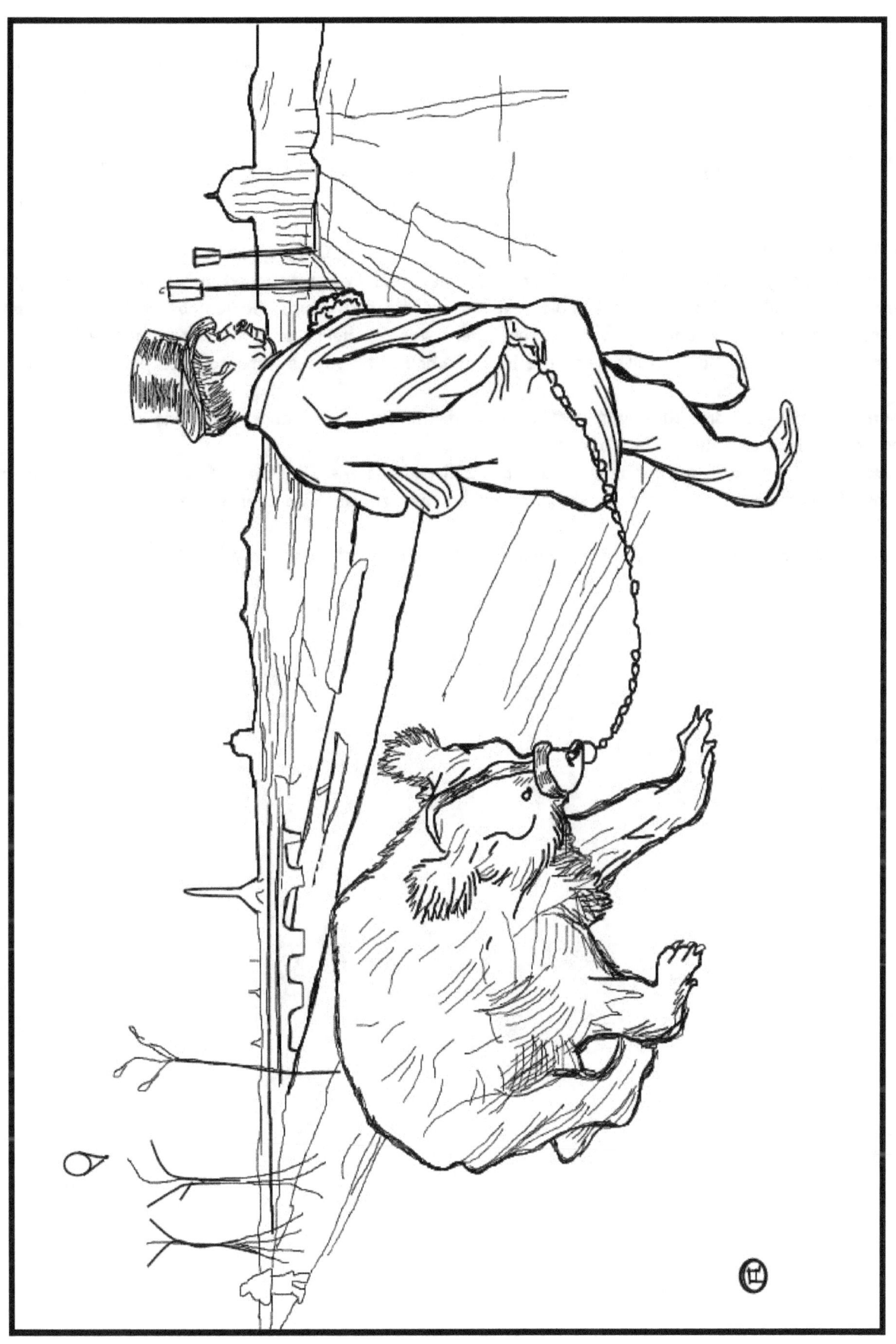

La troupe de Mademoiselle Eglantine
{The Troupe of Miss Eglantine}

The Cancan
"In olden days a glimpse of stockings. Was looked on as something shocking…"
-Cole Porter.

In the England during the height of the Victorian era (1837 to 1901) a glimpse of stocking wasn't only considered shocking by the words like "leg" or "legs" were not even mentioned in respectable society. Legs were even spoken of as "unmentionables" in respectable households. Ladies covered their legs at all times. Skirts were long and big to make sure there was no chance of a leg unmentionable being seen. In later years of the Victorian era the legs of chairs and tables were covered by little skirts.

But then at about the same time on the other side of the Channel a dance was being created that celebrated the lags of ladies. The Cancan.
The Cancan first began to appear in working class ballrooms in the 1830's. It featured women in black stockings lifting their skirts in a teasing manner while they danced in a chorus line.

Jacques Offenbach's music "The Infernal Galop" is the tune usually associated with the Cancan.

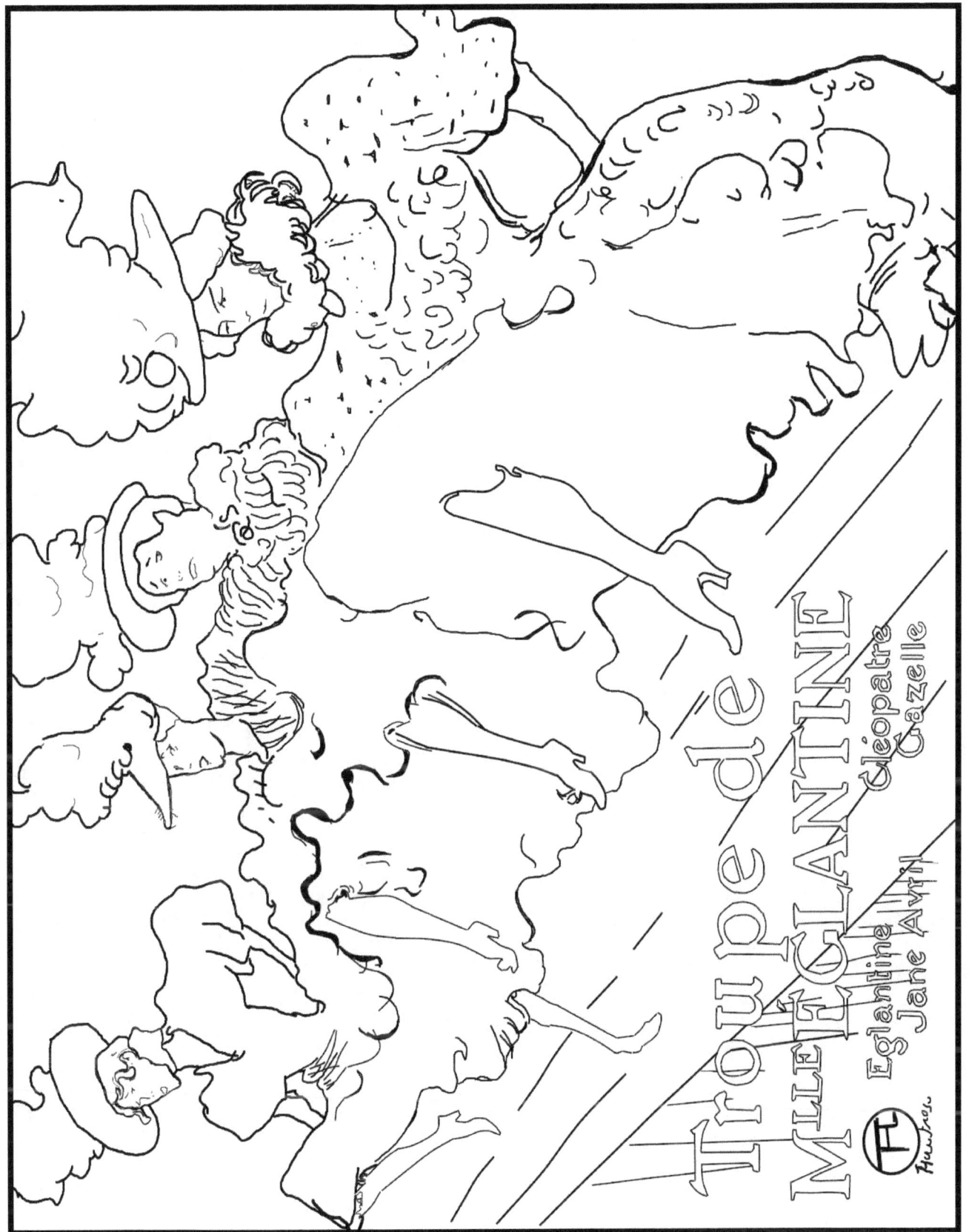

Au Moulin Rouge {At the Moulin Rouge} (1892)
Lautrec can be seen in the distance next to the standing man.

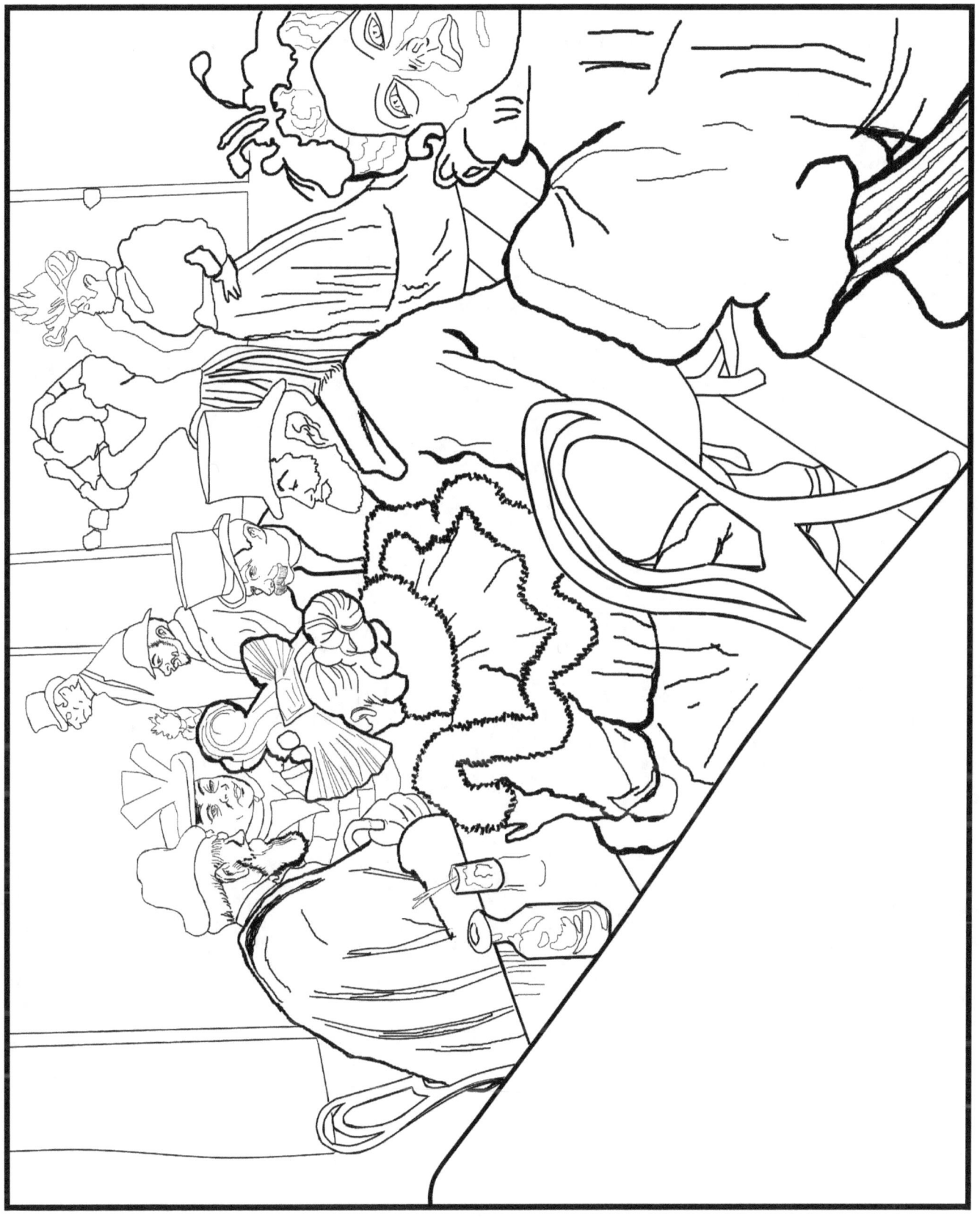

This is the cover of "Babylon of the Germans" a book by "Victor Joze, a friend of Lautrec.

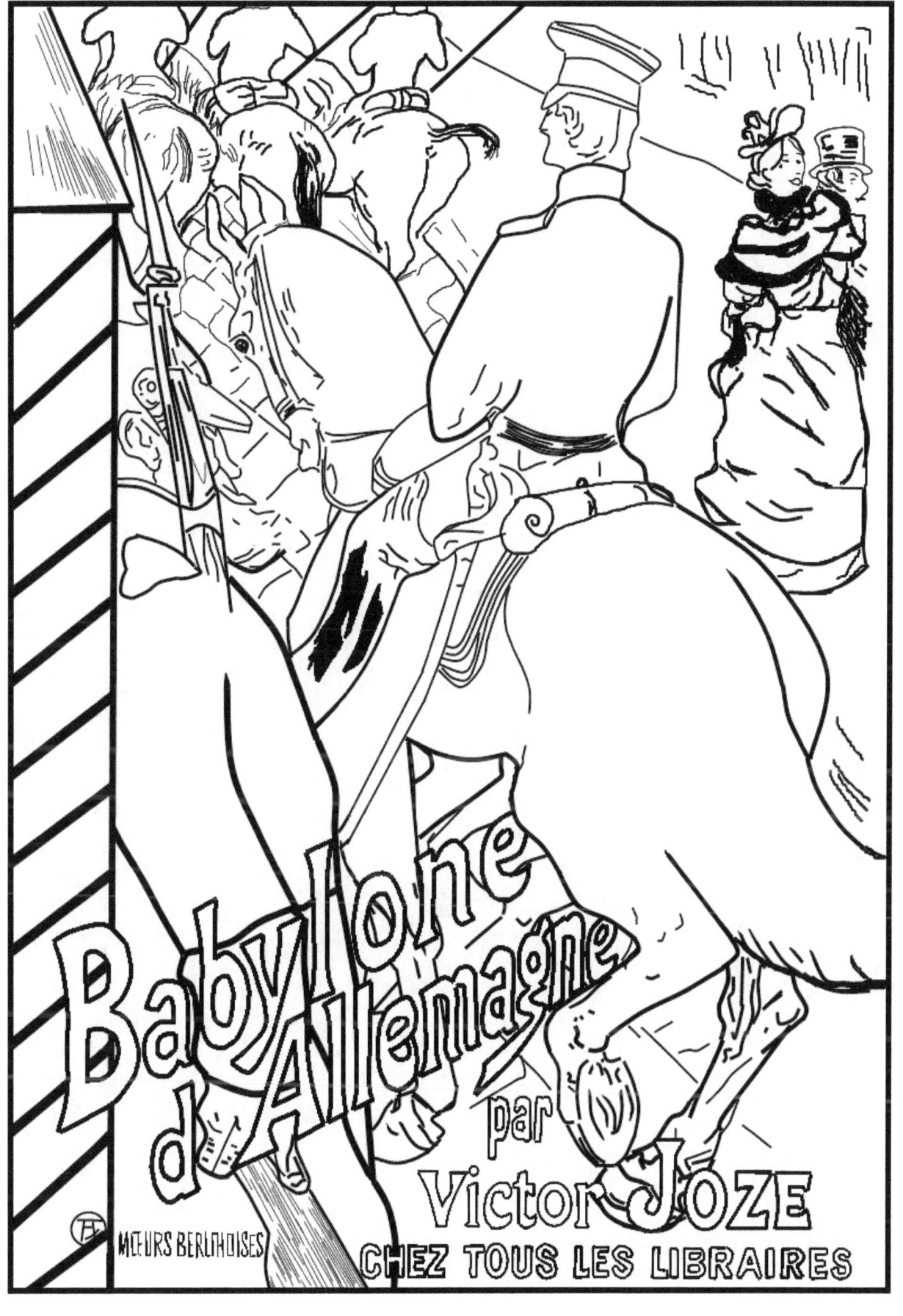

Jane Avril

Jardin de Paris
{Garden of Paris}

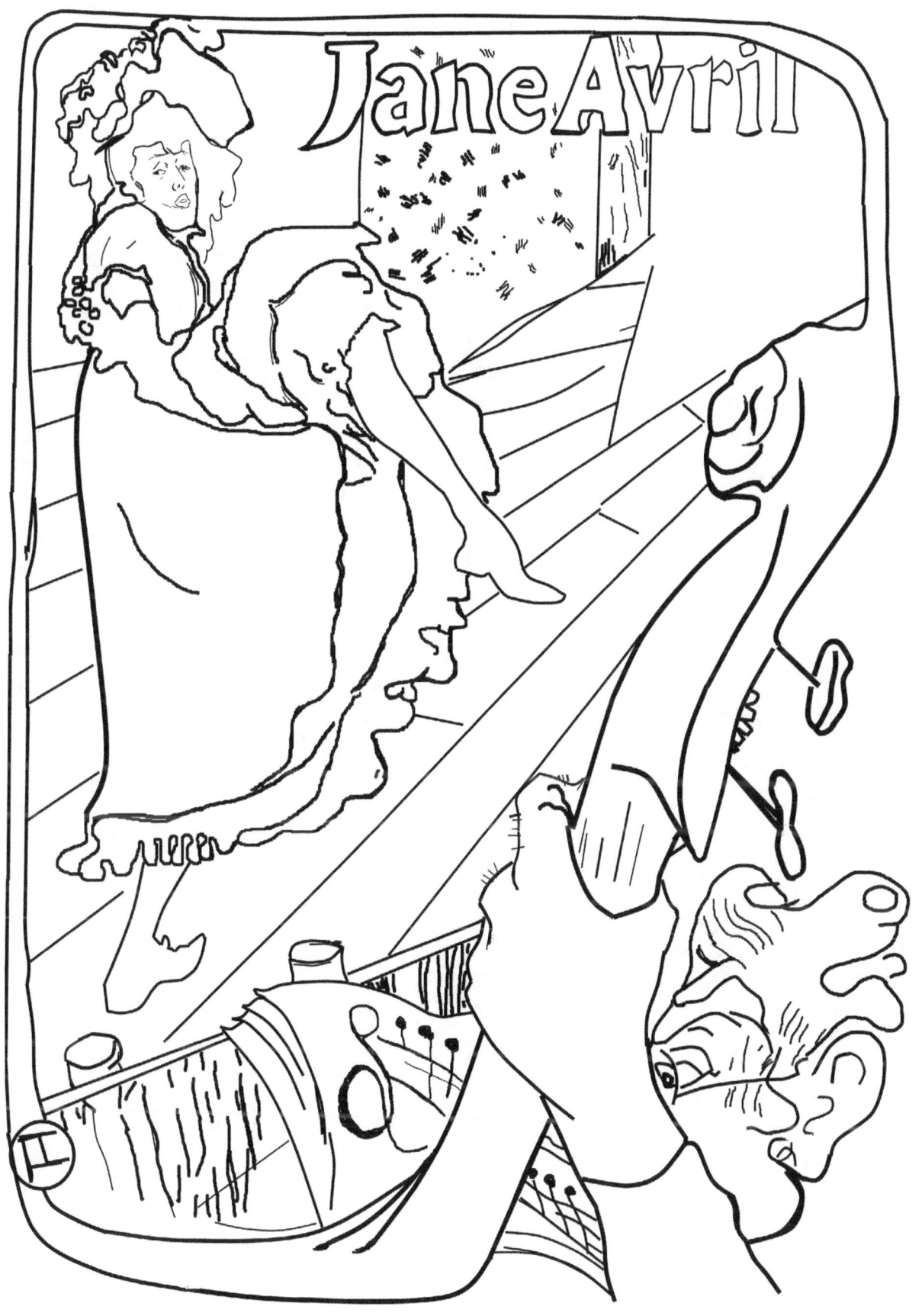

Yvette Guilbert (1865 -1944) Cabaret singer and actress

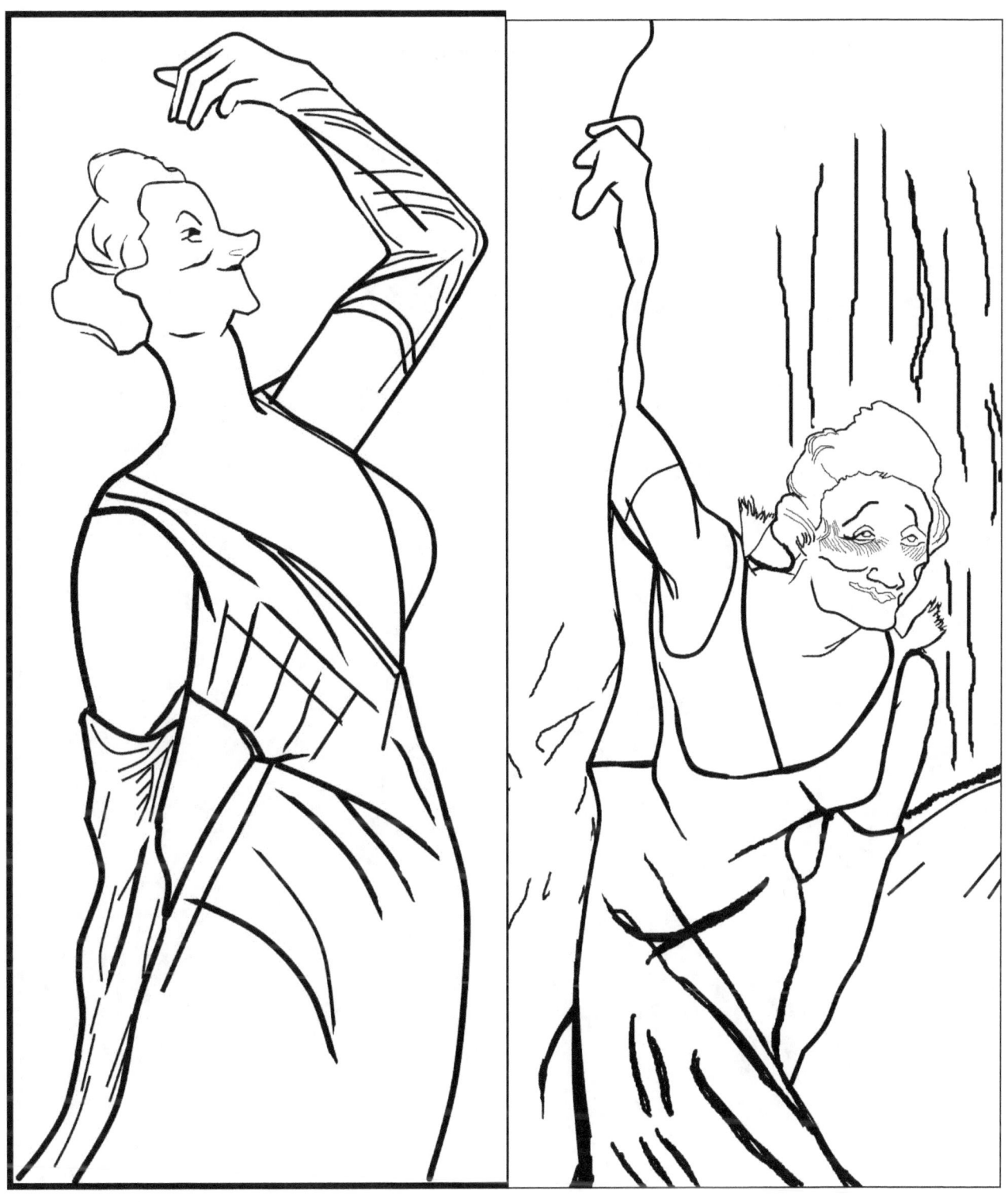

{Japanese divan} Jane Avril sits at her table and watches Yvette Guilbert on stage. 1892

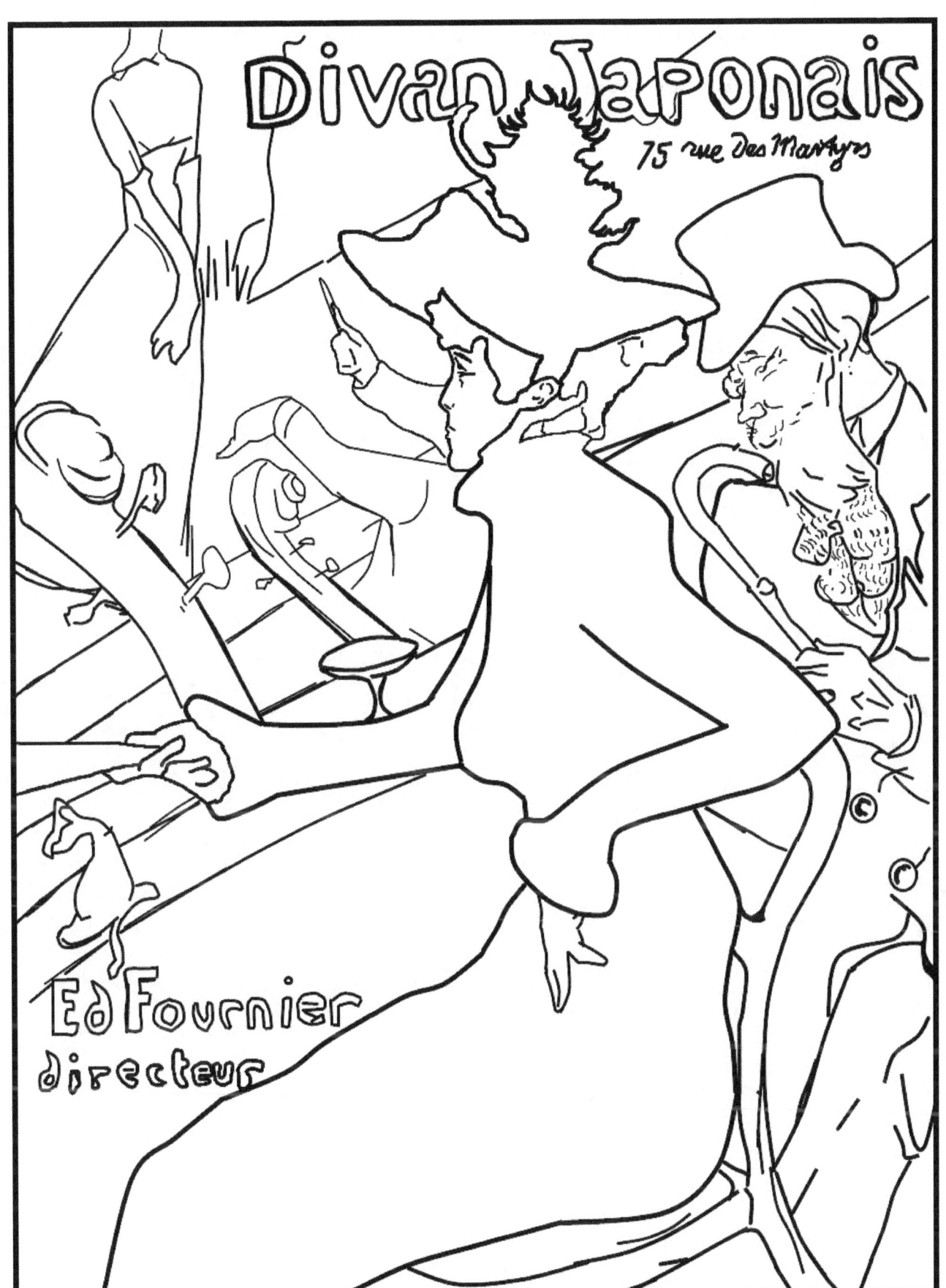

"La danse au Moulin Rouge" {The dance at the Red Mill} 1890

'The Glutton', Louise Weber and Valentin, the 'Boneless One' take center stage as the other patrons watch.

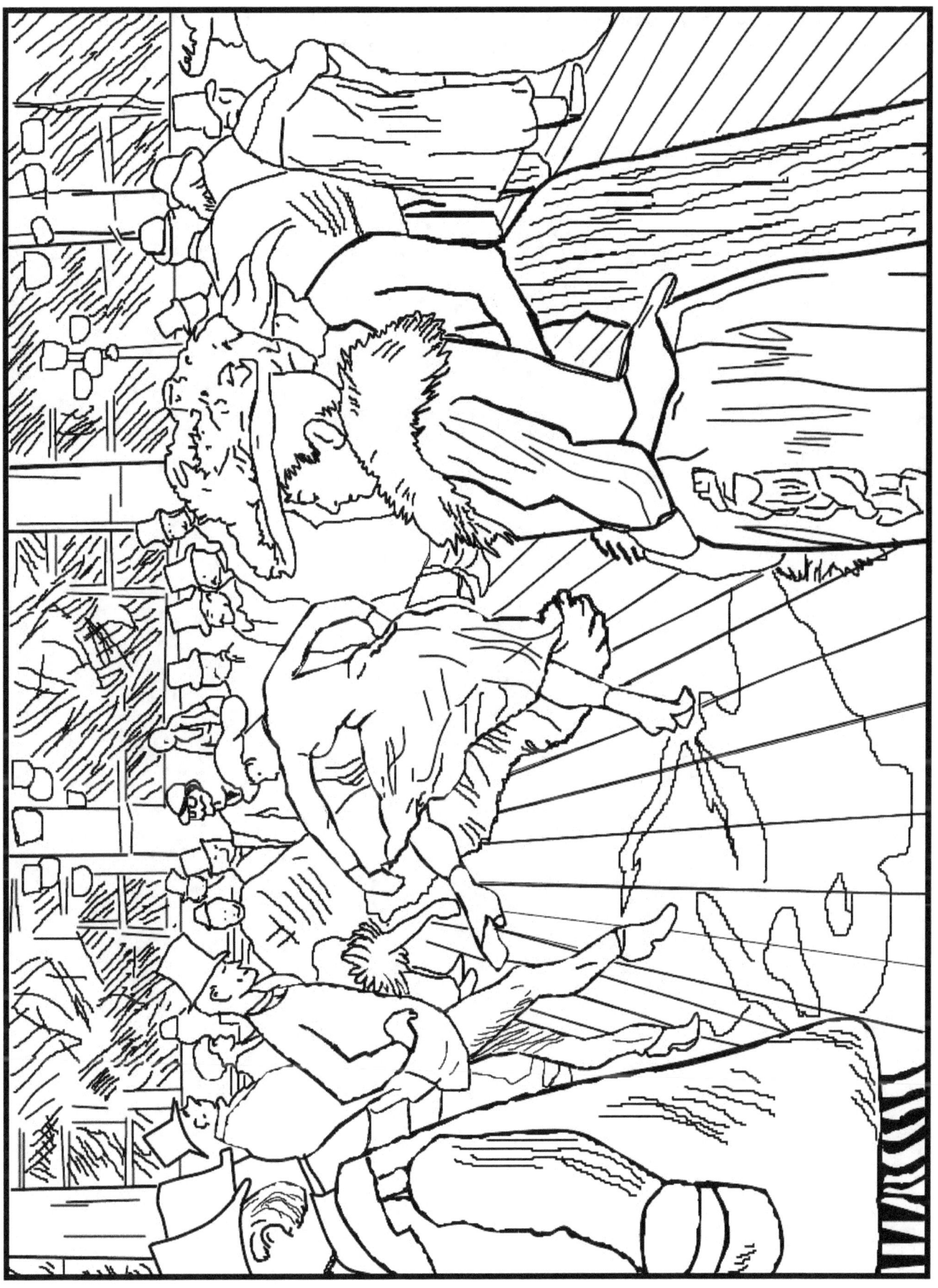

Lautrec painting La danse au Moulin Rouge" {The Dance at the Red Mill} 1890
From photo by Maurice Guibert

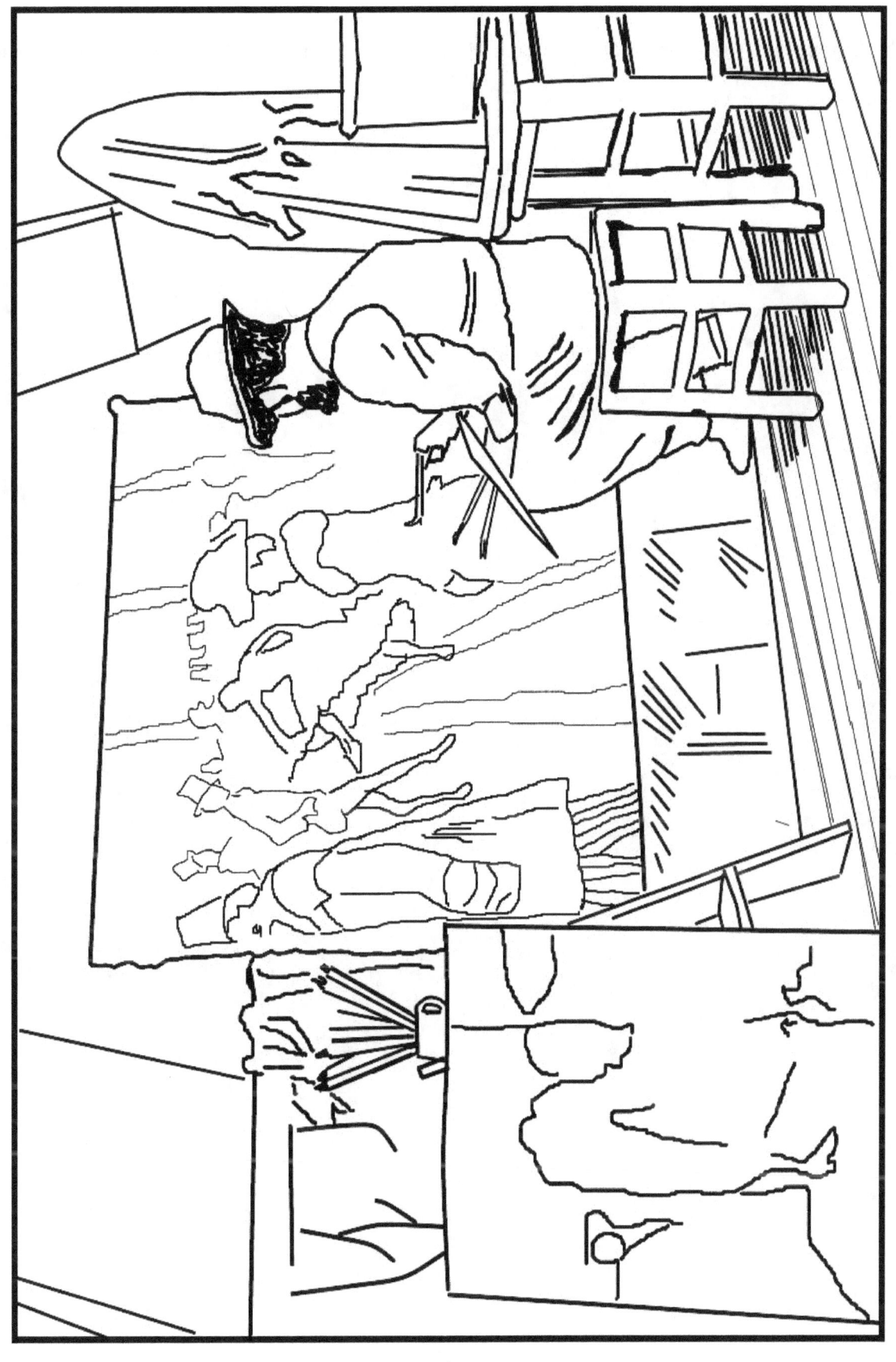

La Chaine Simpson {The Simpson Chain} was a bicycle chain invented by William Spears Simpson in 1895.

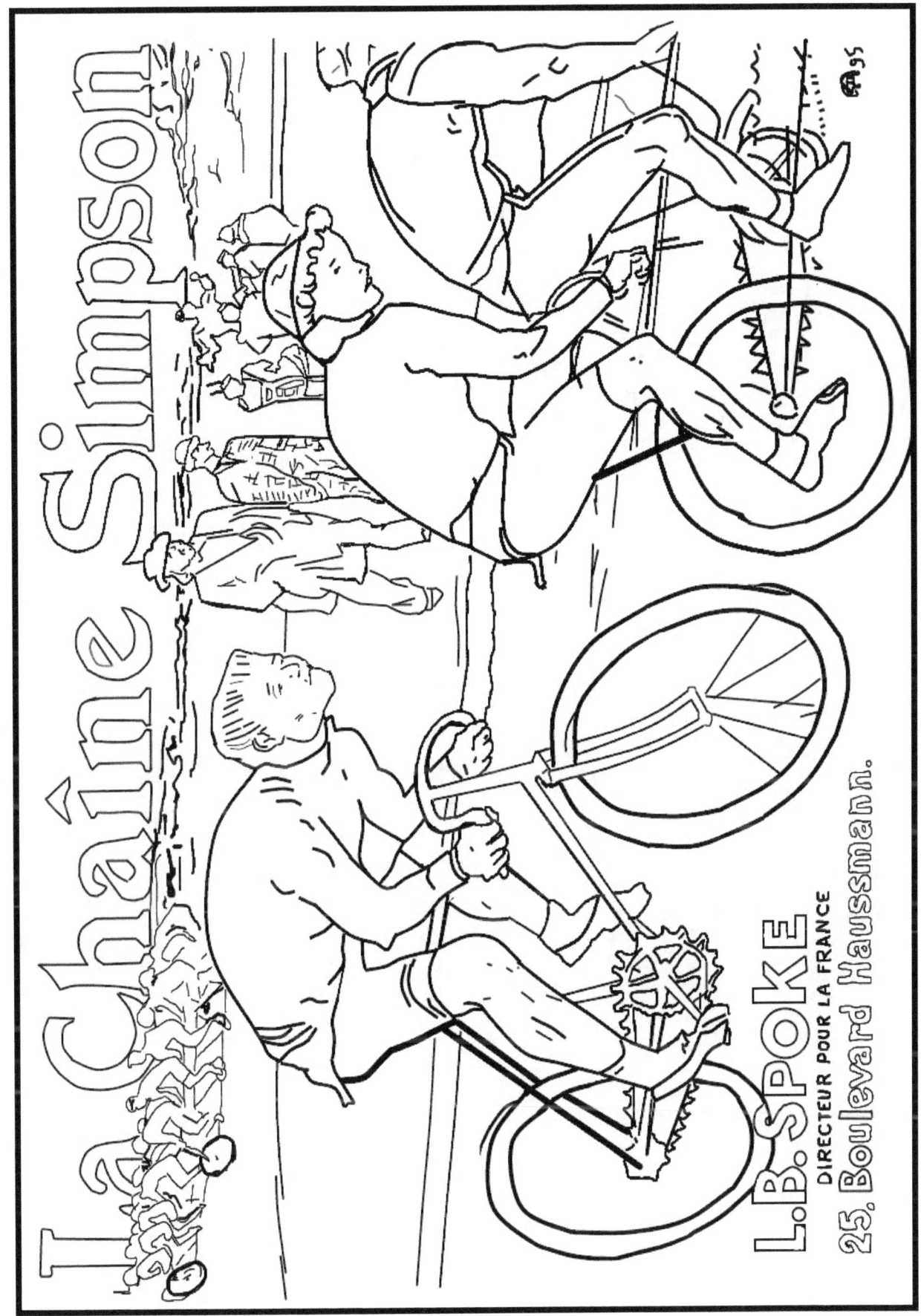

Lautrec often attended the Paris Circus.

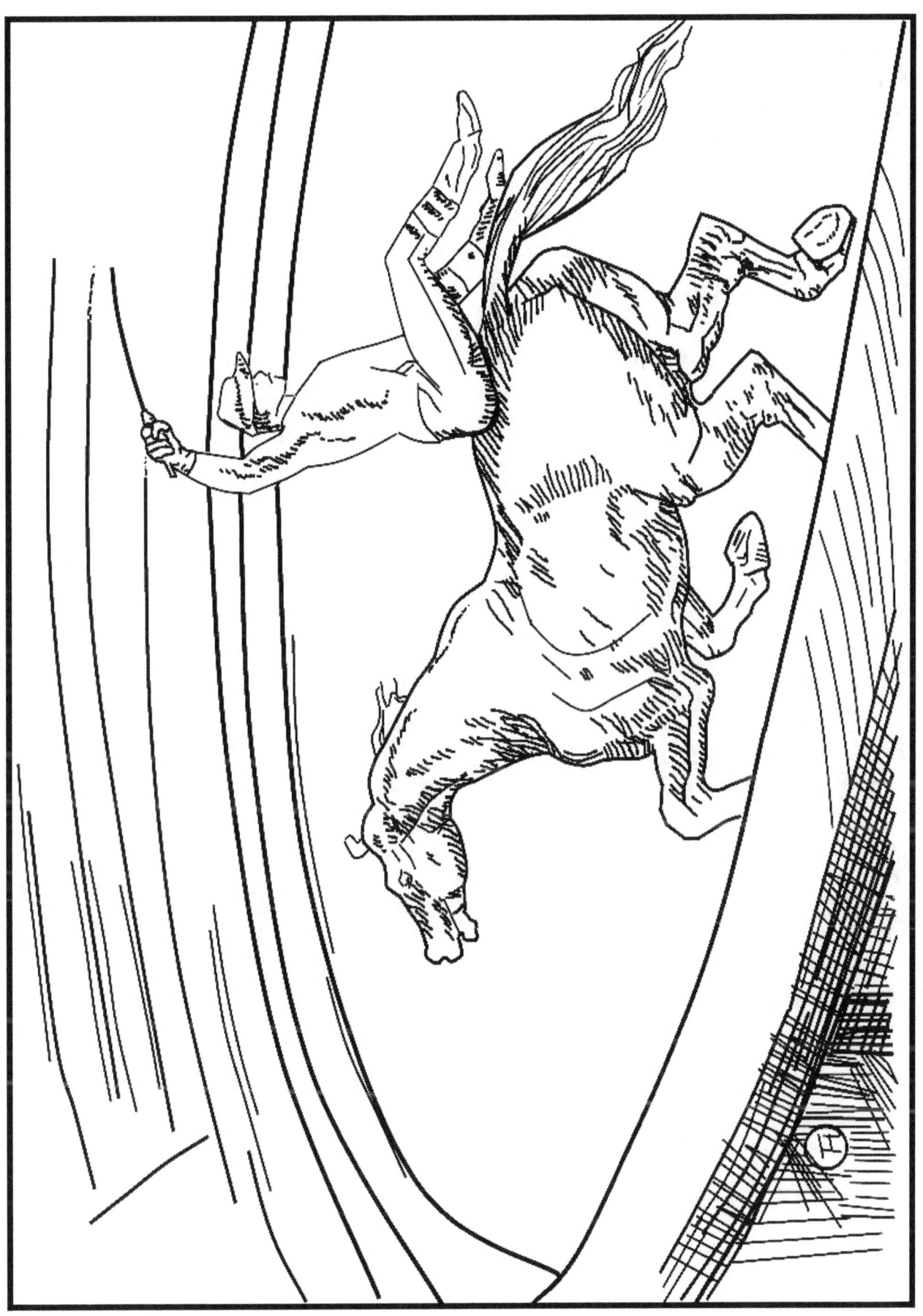

Paul Sescau was a photographer and friend of Lautrec. The lady in the photo is believed to be Jane Avril. 1894.
Sescau had a reputation as a ladies' man who often worked out of his photographic studio;)
The question marks on the subjects dress may be a symbolic jest by Lautrec.

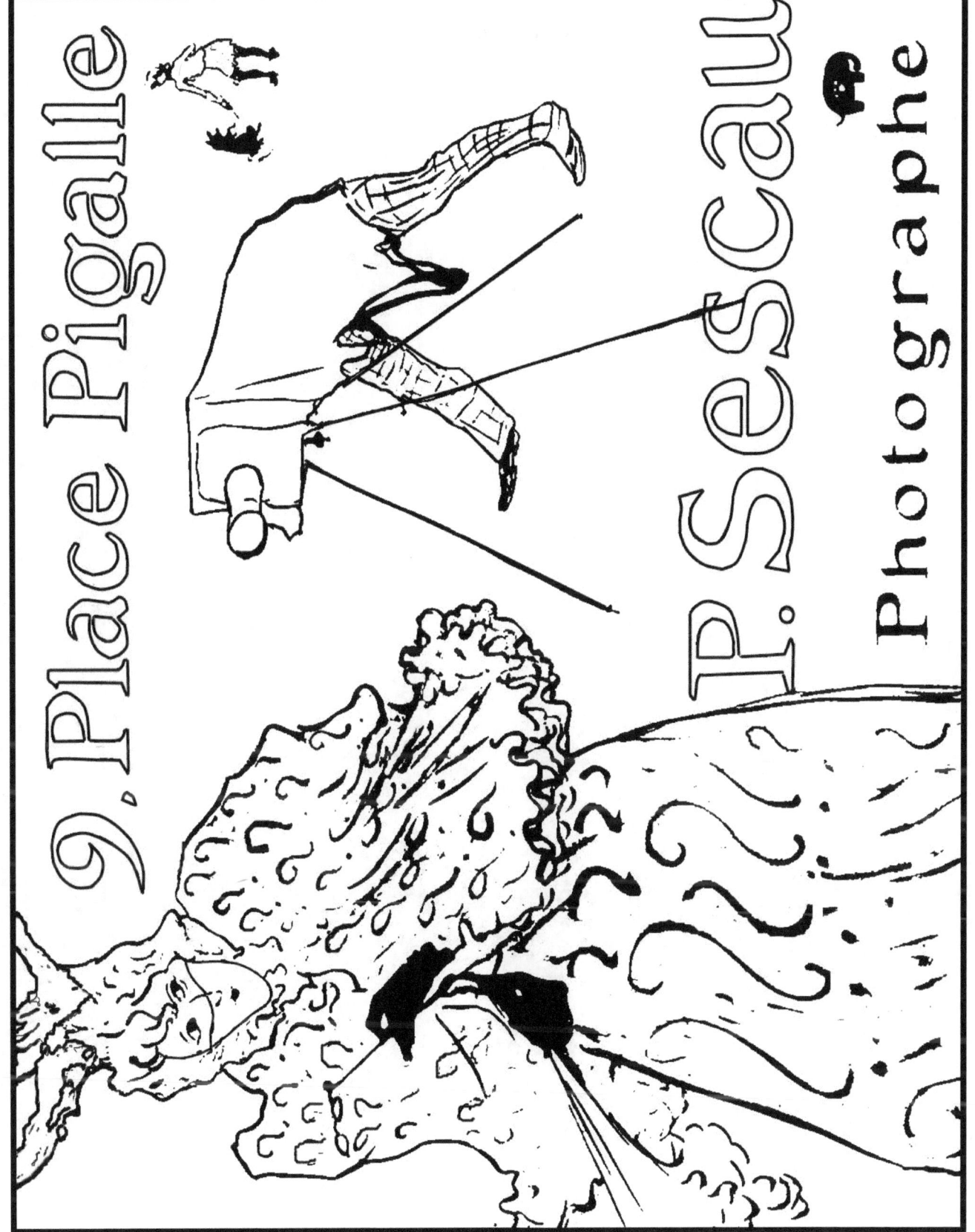

Salon at the Rue des Moulins

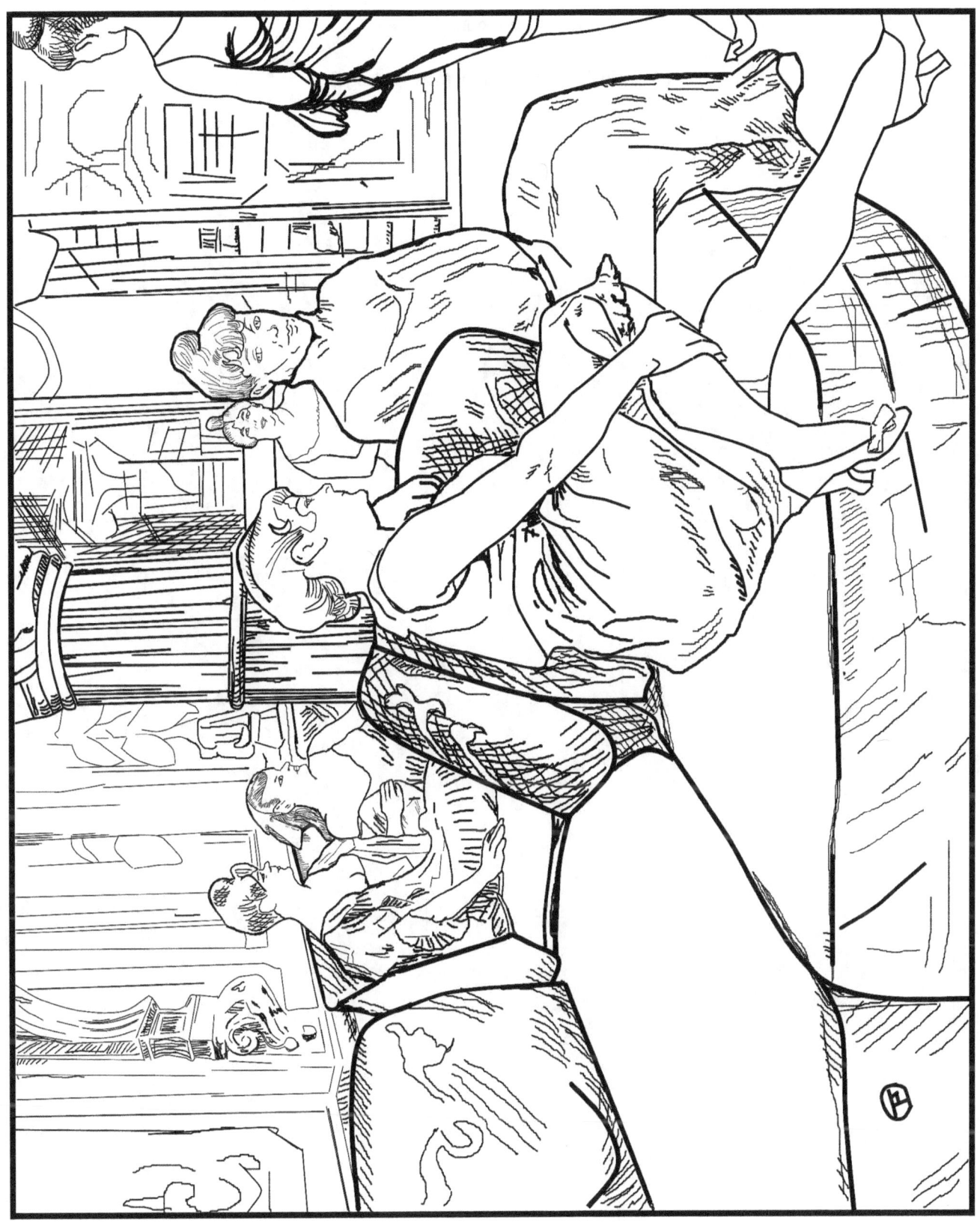

L'anglais au Moulin Rouge

{The Englishman at the Moulin Rouge}

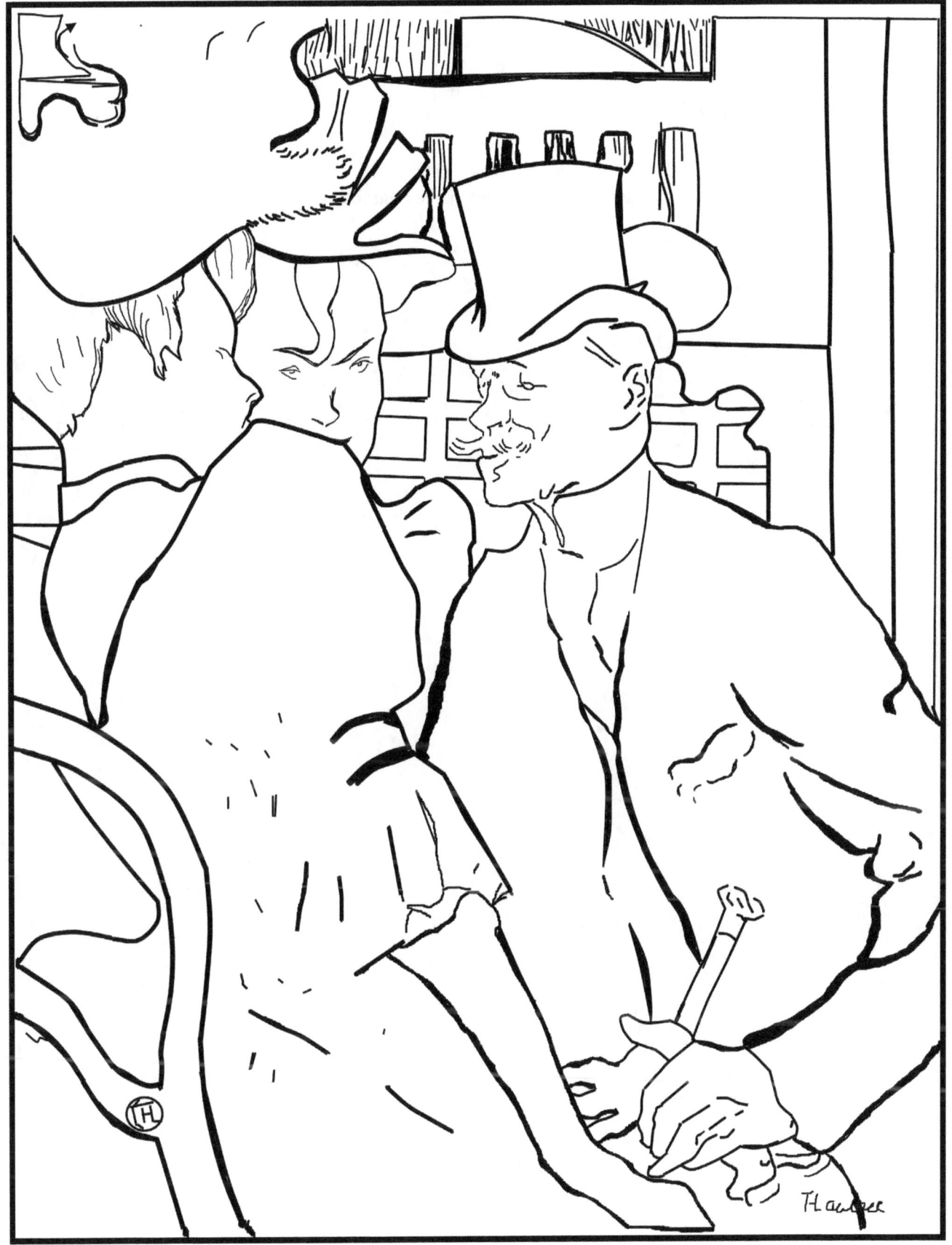

Ta Bouche,
{Your mouth}

Pen and ink sketch
Illustration from Les vieilles Histoires

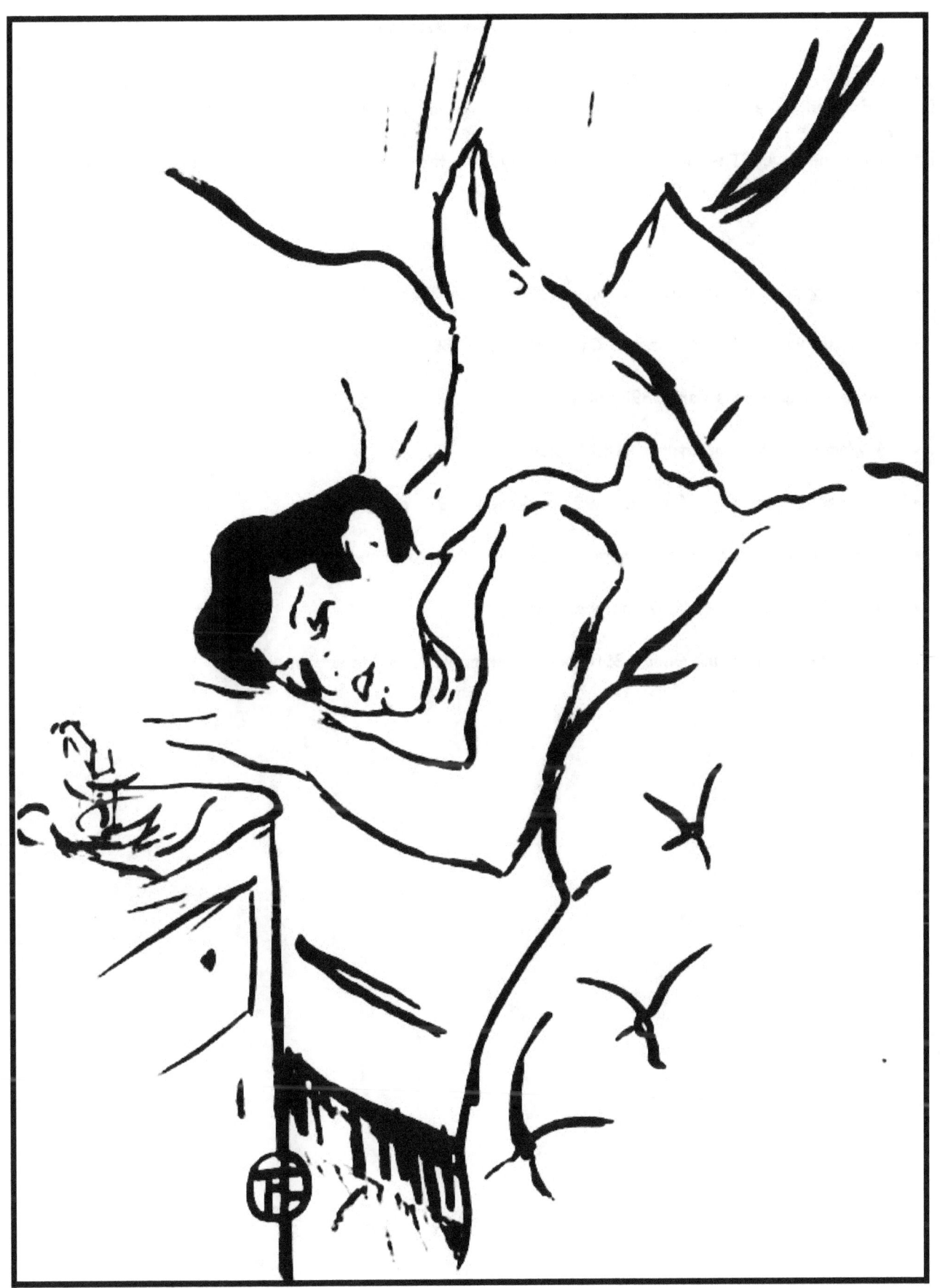

Irish poet, author and playwright Oscar Wilde {1854 – 1900}

Oscar Wilde lived in Paris as exile for the last three years of his life after severing two years in prison in England. Like Lautrec, Wilde was an artistic genius but social misfit not fully appreciated in his time.

Wilde wrote the novel "The Picture of Dorian Gray." At the beginning of the story the Character Dorian Gray is having his picture painted.

Wilde's other works include:

- The Happy Prince and Other Stories (1888, fairy stories)

- Lord Arthur Savile's Crime and Other Stories (1891, stories)

- Lady Windermere's Fan (1892, play)

- A Woman of No Importance (1893, play)

- An Ideal Husband (performed 1895, published 1898; play)

- The Importance of Being Earnest (performed 1895, published 1898; play)

- De Profundis (written 1897; an open letter)

- The Ballad of Reading Gaol (1898, poem written while Wilde was in prison)

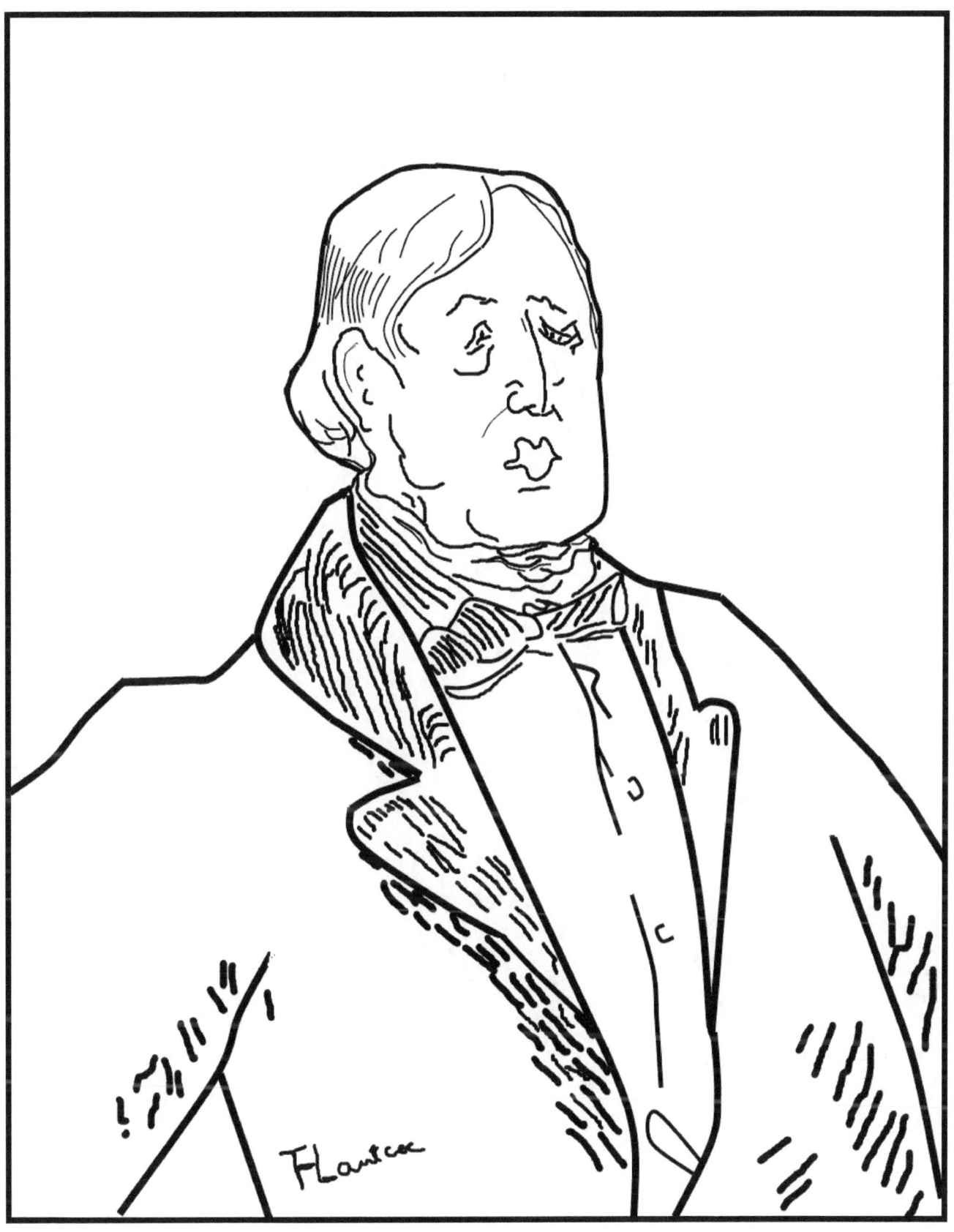

Pen and ink sketch

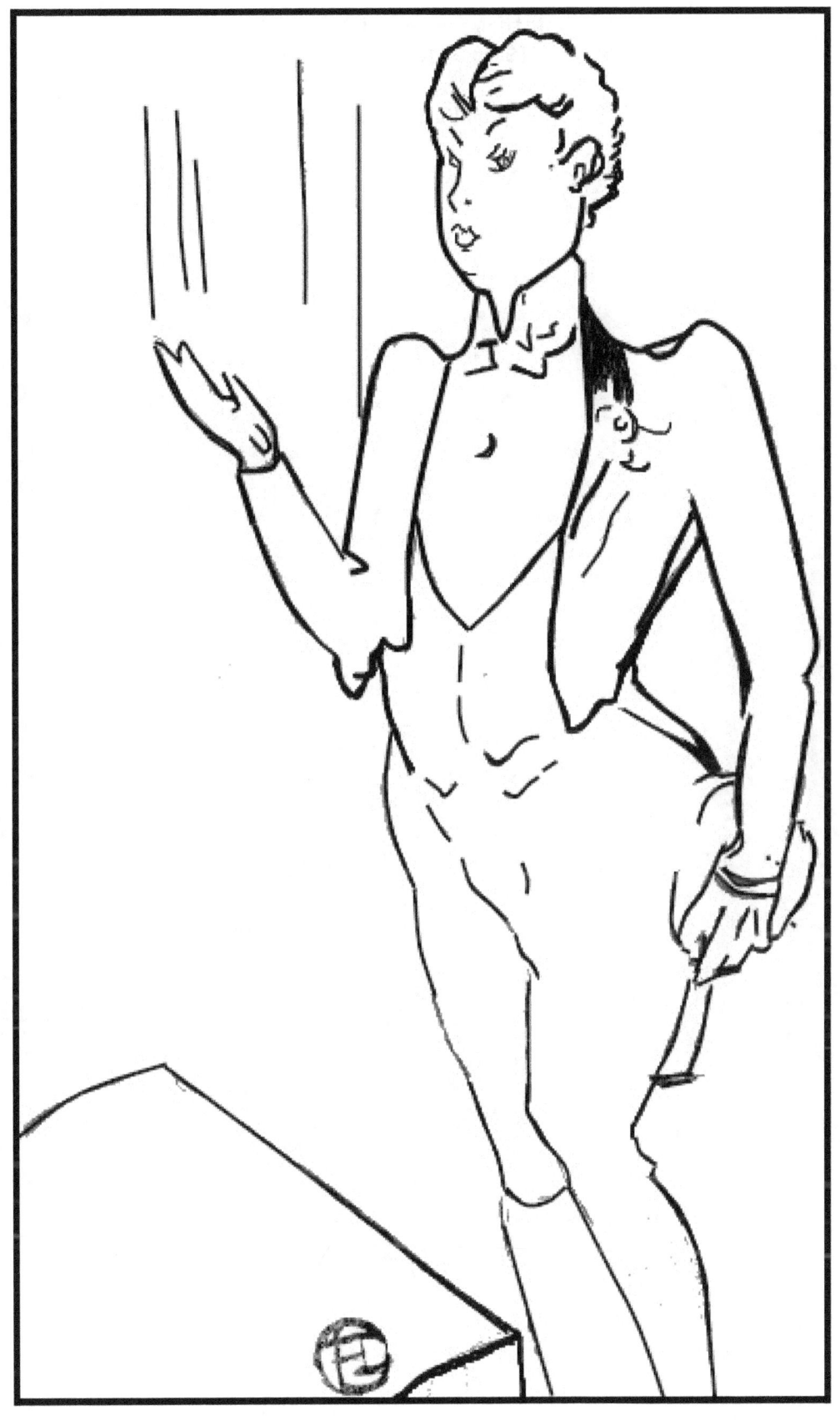

An illustration for "A Saint Lazare"
(Song Title) 1892

Pen and ink sketch

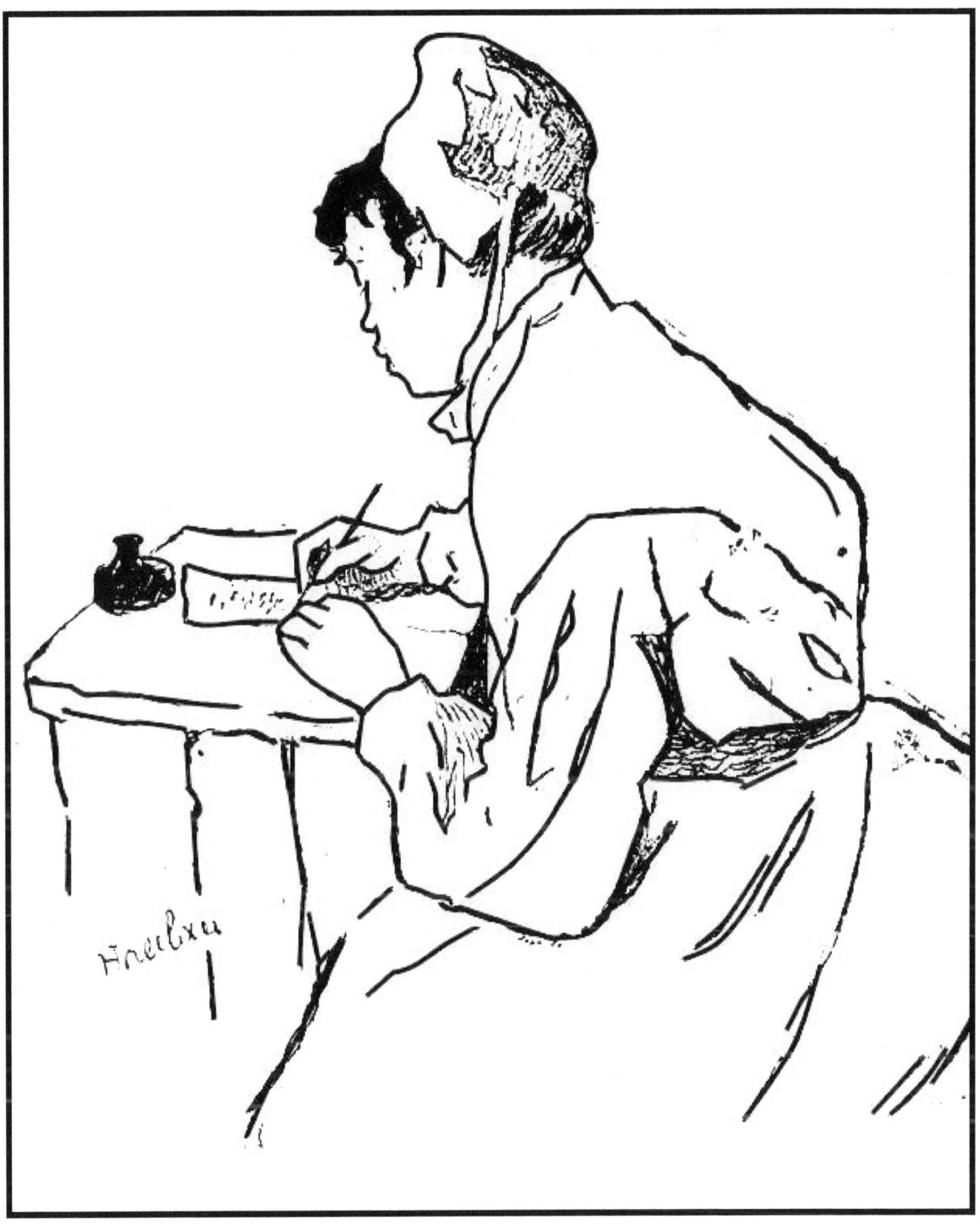

Irish and American Bar, Rue Royale - The Chap Book

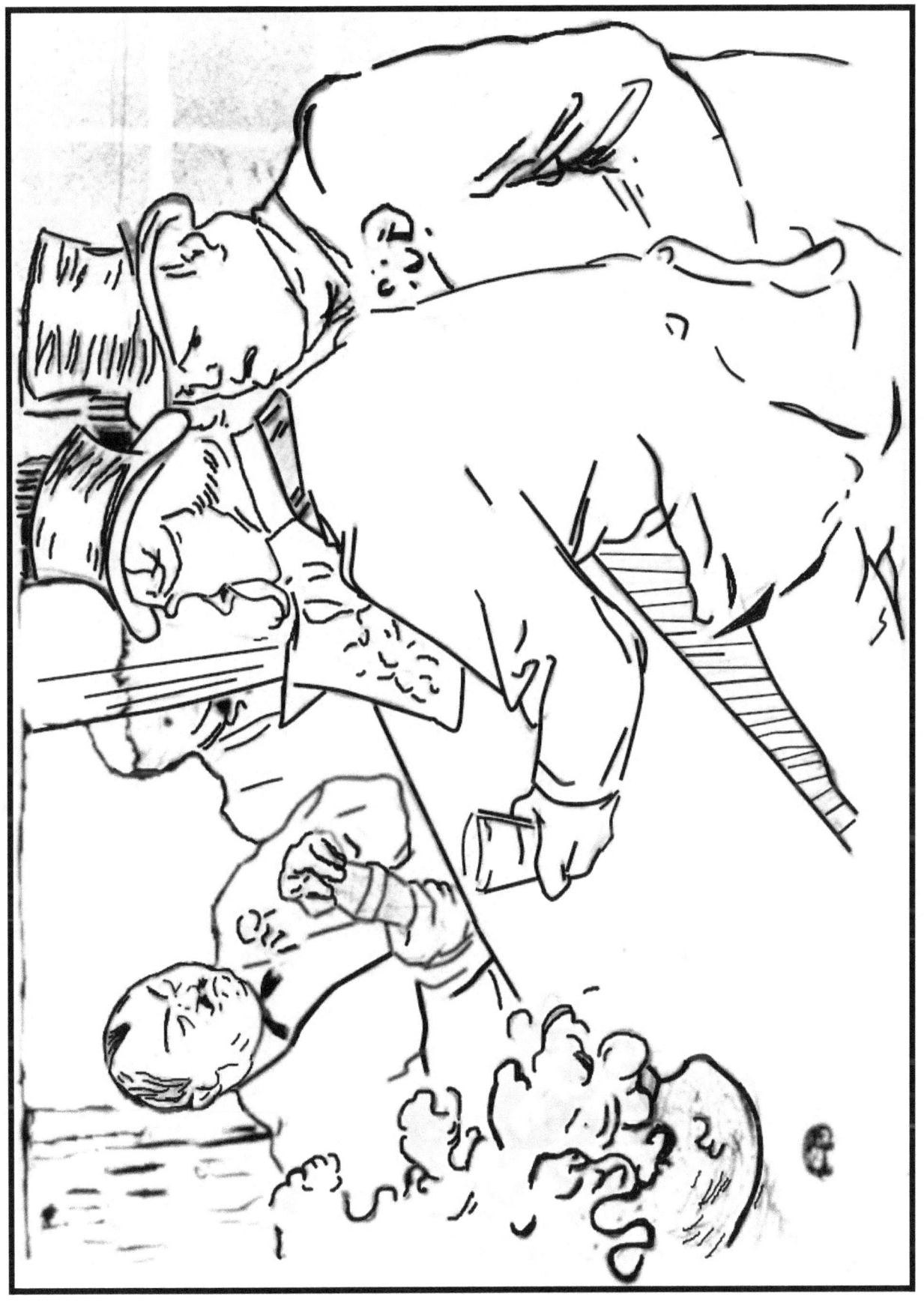

Gueule de bois
ou
Le buveur

{Hangover
Or
The Drinker}

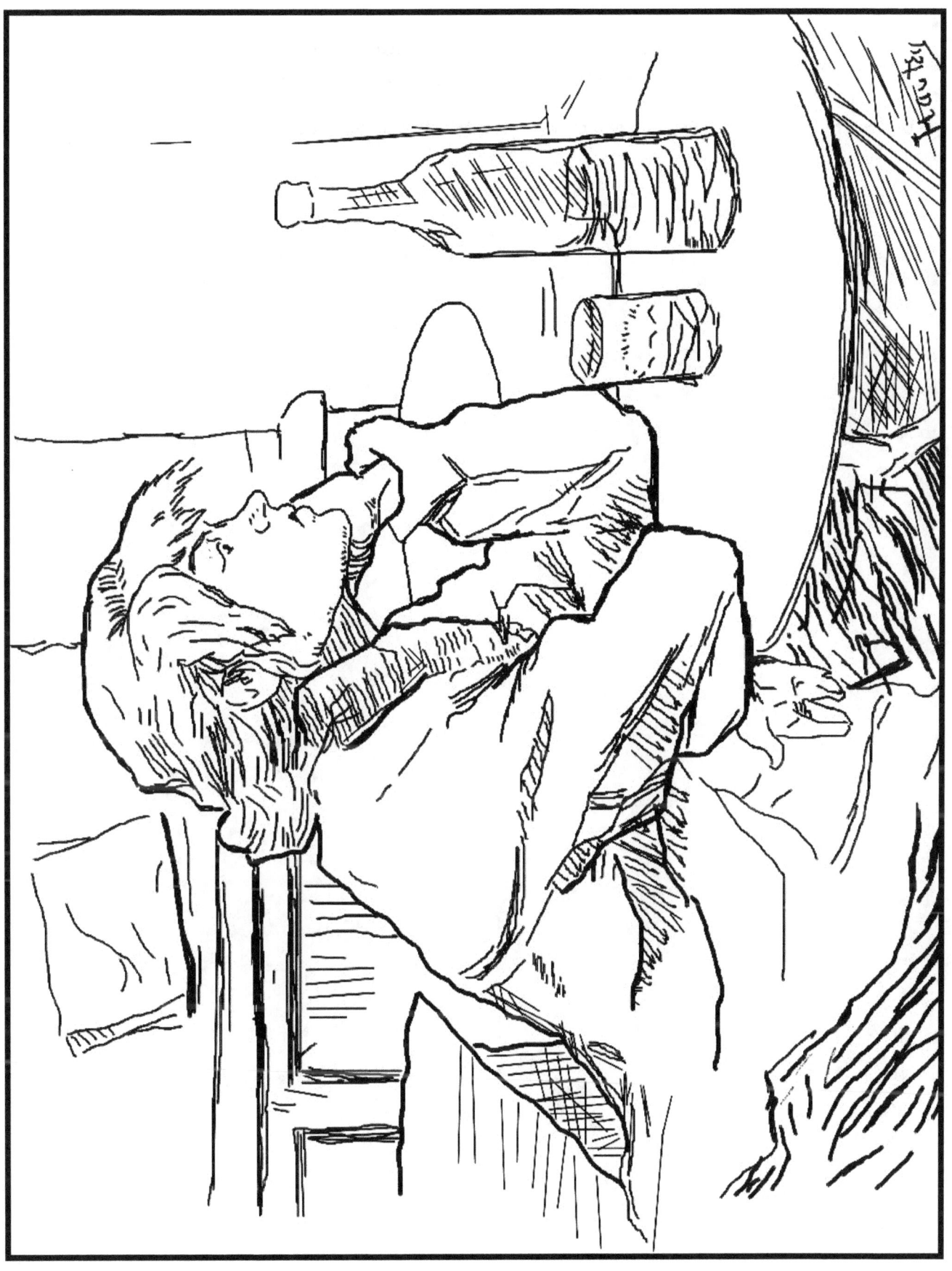

La Clownesse Cha-U-Kao au Moulin Rouge.
{The lady clown Cha-U-Kao at the Moulin Rouge}

Cha-U-Kao (that was her name) was one of the first female clowns. (1895)

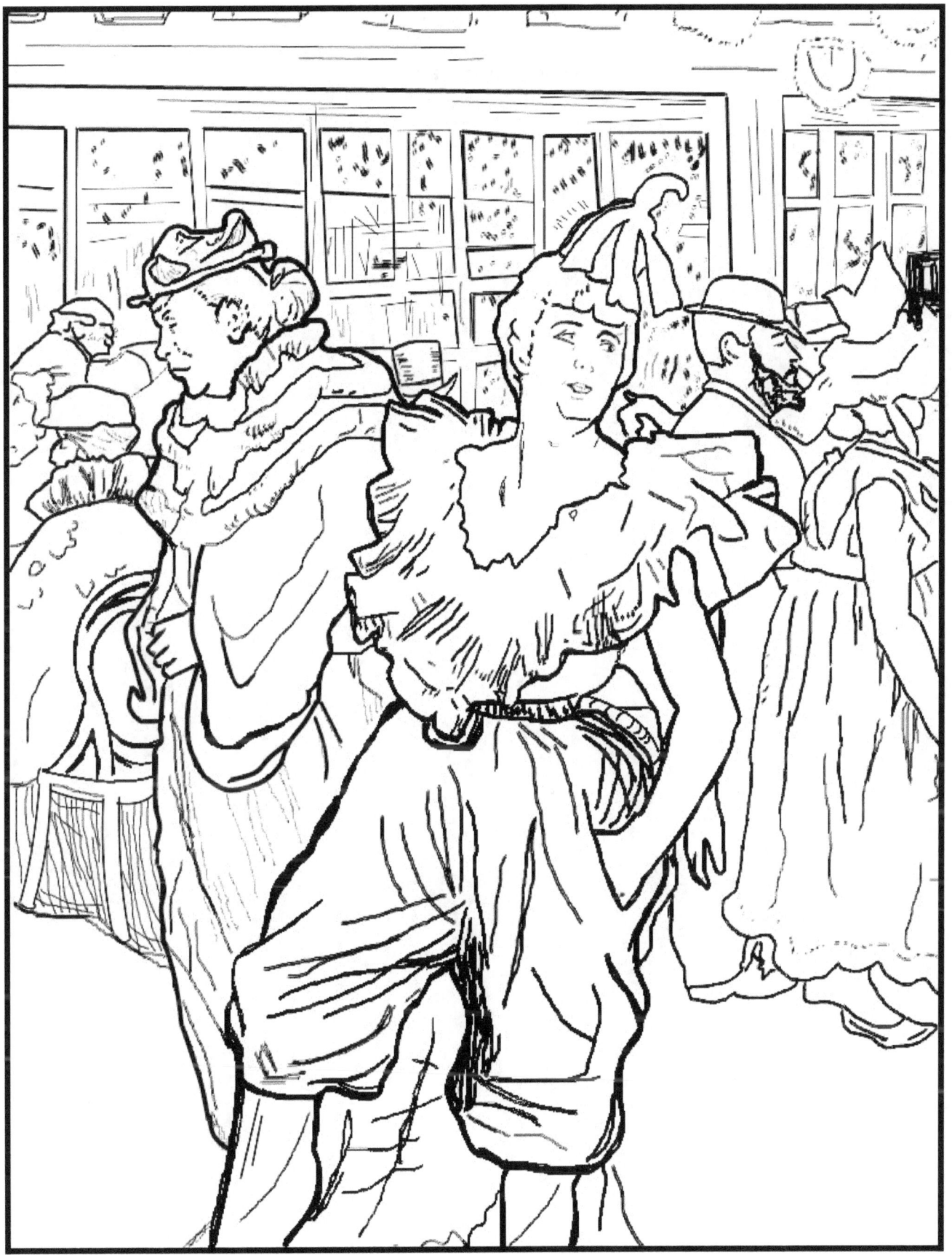

Confetti 1894

Manufactured j e bella

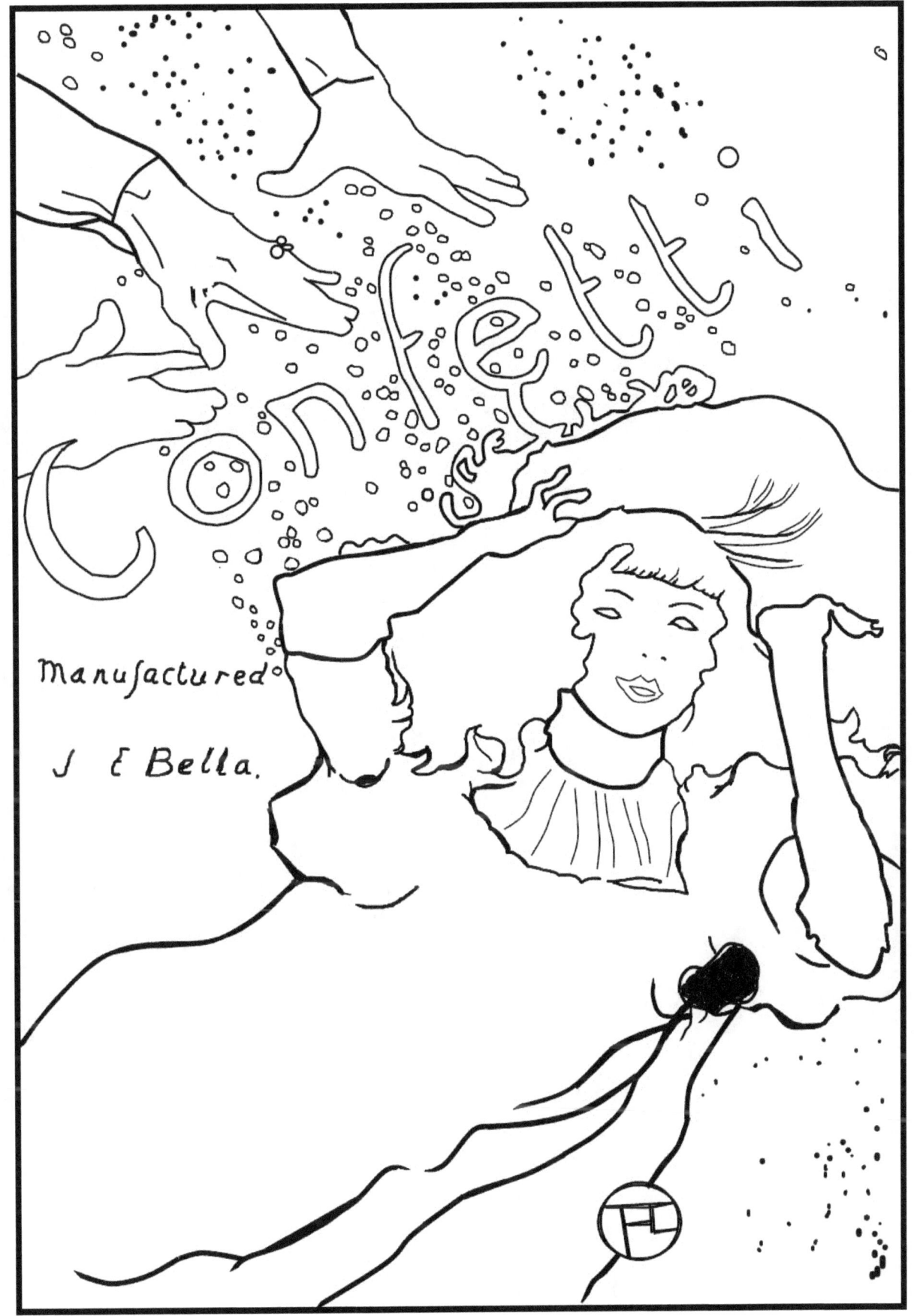

www.ingramcontent.com/pod-product-compliance
Lightning Source LLC
Chambersburg PA
CBHW080607180526

45168CB00007B/2808